FROM REVIE~
PRE~

"Eric Maisel's psychologic

~wrary Journal

"Eric Maisel has made a career out of helping artists cope with the traumas and troubles that are the price of admission to a creative life."

— *Intuition* magazine

"Eric Maisel's books should be required reading for anyone involved in the arts, especially students and their teachers. Maisel demystifies the process of creating art."

— *Theatre Design and Technology Journal*

PRAISE FOR *BRAINSTORM* BY ERIC MAISEL AND ANN MAISEL

"[*Brainstorm*] is a book that should be read by all who want to live their life in a way that is vital and leaves some kind of legacy. It's not about fame and fortune, but rather, about ensuring that this brief span that we have on Earth is one that has value — where we leave some kind of impression. There's nothing that matters more."

— *Seattle Post-Intelligencer*

"All too often people overlook the basics of a productive life, distracted by multitasking, marketing, and information overload. With this provocative departure from the usual lifestyle manual, the Maisels are out to break us of those tendencies."

— *Publishers Weekly*

"Presents a new way of thinking about how to turn brain potential into passion, energy, and genuine accomplishments."
— Camille Minichino, physicist and author of the Periodic Table Mysteries

"What a pivotal way to experience your brain and all that it can create! I love that this book celebrates and teaches the concept of productive obsession and the multitudinous gifts of brainstorming."
— SARK, artist and author of *Glad No Matter What* and other books (www.PlanetSARK.com)

"A great tool for anyone who might be feeling stuck with a creative urge or idea but hasn't brought it to fruition. You'll discover how to use your brain as your ally and go beyond what you thought possible."
— Phyllis Lane, documentary filmmaker

"Elegantly combines the most inspiring elements of mindfulness, engagement, focus, and flow. Eric Maisel shows how we can be more productive by turning obsessions into positive passions."
— Susan K. Perry, PhD, social psychologist, author of *Writing in Flow*, and creativity blogger for *Psychology Today*

"You need to buy this book now, let it liberate your spirit, and put the Maisels' plan into practice. Then buy copies for every creative person you know. It's absolutely the finest gift you could ever give."
— Jed Diamond, PhD, author of *Mr. Mean: Saving Your Relationship from the Irritable Male Syndrome* and *Male Menopause*

MASTERING
CREATIVE
ANXIETY

ALSO BY ERIC MAISEL

MASTERING CREATIVE ANXIETY

24 LESSONS
for Writers, Painters, Musicians & Actors
from America's Foremost Creativity Coach

ERIC MAISEL

New World Library
Novato, California

New World Library
14 Pamaron Way
Novato, California 94949

Text design by Tona Pearce Myers

Library of Congress Cataloging-in-Publication Data
Maisel, Eric, date.
Mastering creative anxiety : twenty-four lessons for writers, painters, musicians, and actors from America's foremost creativity coach / Eric Maisel.
    p.   cm.
Includes bibliographical references and index.
ISBN 978-1-57731-932-0 (pbk. : alk. paper)
  1. Creative ability. 2. Anxiety. 3. Performance anxiety. 4. Writer's block.
5. Artists—Psychology. I. Title.
BF408.M2326 2011
700.1'9—dc22   2010048857

First printing, March 2011
ISBN 978-1-57731-932-0
Printed in Canada on 100% postconsumer-waste recycled paper

New World Library is a proud member of the Green Press Initiative.

10 9 8 7 6 5 4 3 2

CONTENTS

INTRODUCTION

Are you creating less often than you would like? Are you avoiding your creative work altogether? If so, anxiety may be the culprit! Anxiety regularly stops creative people in their tracks and makes their experience of creating more painful than pleasurable. It stops would-be creative people entirely, preventing them from realizing their dreams. Anxiety is the number one problem that creative people face — and yet few even realize it.

Do you procrastinate? That's anxiety. Do you resist getting to your work or marketing your work? That's anxiety. Do you have trouble deciding which creative project to tackle? That's anxiety. Do you find completing work hard? That's anxiety. Anxiety permeates the creative process. Learn what to do about it! In this book you'll learn how to start and complete your creative projects without experiencing disabling anxiety.

You'll learn little-known anxiety-management techniques that can help enormously. And you'll also learn what *not* to do in dealing with creative anxiety.

In these twenty-four lessons I'll describe many of the sources of anxiety in a creative person's life and provide you with an anxiety mastery menu of strategies and techniques to help you manage that anxiety. The more you understand these sources of anxiety and learn how to hone your anxiety-management skills, the better you'll be able to deal with the rigors of the creative process and the realities of the creative life. Get ready to create calmly!

CHAPTER 1

THE ANXIETY OF CREATING AND NOT CREATING

nxiety is part of the human condition. And it is a much larger part than most people realize. A great deal of what we do in life we do to reduce our experience of anxiety or to avoid anxiety altogether. Our very human defensiveness is one of the primary ways that we avoid experiencing anxiety. If something is about to make us anxious we deny that it is happening, make ourselves sick so that we can concentrate on our sickness, get angry at our mate so as to have something else to focus on, and so on. We are very tricky creatures in this regard.

We are also very wonderful creatures who have it in us to create. *Creativity* is the word we use for our desire to make use of our inner resources, employ our imagination, knit together our thoughts and feelings into beautiful things such as songs, quilts, or novels, and feel like the hero of our own story. It is the way that we make manifest our potential, make use of our intelligence, and embrace what we love. When we create, we feel whole, useful, and devoted. Unfortunately, we often also feel anxious as we create or contemplate creating. There are many reasons for this — the subject of our twenty-four lessons. We get anxious because we fear failing, because we fear disappointing ourselves, because the work can be extremely hard, because the marketplace may criticize us and reject us. We want to create, but we also don't want to create so as to spare ourselves all this anxiety. That is the simple, profound dilemma that millions of people find themselves in.

The solution sounds very simple but is much harder to put into practice. To create and to deal with all the anxiety that comes with creating, you must acknowledge and accept that anxiety is part of the process, demand of yourself that you will learn — and really practice! — anxiety-management skills so that you can master the anxiety that arises, and get on with your creating and your anxiety management. It is too tragic not to create if creating is what you long to do, and there is no reason for you not to create if "all" that is standing in the way is your quite human, very ordinary experience of anxiety. It is time to become an anxiety expert and get on with your creating!

HEADLINE

Since both creating and not creating produce anxiety in anyone who wants to create, you might as well embrace the fact that anxiety will accompany you on your journey as a creative person — whether or not you are getting on with your work. Just embracing that reality will release a lot of the ambient anxiety that you feel. Since anxiety accompanies both states — creating and not creating — why not choose creating?

☑ TO DO

Pick your next creative project or return to your current one with a new willingness to accept the reality of anxiety. To help reduce your experience of anxiety, remember to breathe deeply, speak positively to yourself, and affirm that your creative life matters to you. If some anxiety remains, create anyway!

AND

Use the anxiety mastery menu at the end of this lesson. This work will richly reward you. Making a real effort to deal with your anxiety will allow you to get on with your creating and to create deeply and regularly.

VOW

I will create, even if doing so provokes anxiety; and when it does, I will manage it through the use of the anxiety-management skills and techniques I am learning and practicing.

TEACHING TALE

Each lesson in this book comes with a teaching tale that illustrates the lesson's point. The following teaching tale features Ari, a fictional creativity coach who lives and works in an unnamed desert location. Modeled on Sufi teaching tales, these tales employ naturalistic and fantastic elements and present a moral at the end. Enjoy!

THE GHOST WITH CONSCIOUSNESS AND POTENTIAL

One day a ghost paid Ari a visit. The ghost had long blond hair and wore a banana-colored satin nightgown. Even though she had the power to interrupt and to come and go as she pleased, she arrived between creativity coaching sessions as a gesture of respect and goodwill.

"I never got to use my talents!" the ghost wailed. She floated about the room, agitated and unable to alight. "Now I'm dead and buried!"

"You can't create where you find yourself these days?" Ari asked the miserable ghost.

"No! I just wander the universe, pointlessly and aimlessly!"

"But you sound like you still have a brain?"

That seemed to surprise the ghost. She shot out of the air and sat down suddenly.

"That's true," she replied.

"And you can talk to people?"

"Yes."

"Then why not be a muse?"

"A muse," she murmured. For an instant she looked happy. But then a new thought creased her brow. "Since I never manifested my own potential, how can I help others?"

"Just by telling the truth. Are ghosts more honest than the next person?"

"Not particularly."

"Too bad. But that was an honest thing for you to say! So it appears that you can tell the truth. So, if I were you, I would think about why I hadn't been able to create while I was alive, I would learn the painful truth about that, and then I would visit people who are despairing and help them."

The ghost fell silent.

"I'm drawing a blank," she finally said, "about why I avoided creating my whole life long. Not that it was such a long life!" she interjected suddenly. "I died at thirty-nine."

Ari nodded. "But if it had been sixty-nine or eighty-nine —"

"No, you're right. I was not on the path to creating. I could have lived another fifty years, and I wouldn't have accomplished anything."

She flew off the chair and circled the room ten or fifteen times. Ari, watching her, began to get dizzy.

"Come down here!" he cried. "Settle down for a moment!"

The ghost dove to her seat and sat there hunched and moody.

"For a lifetime you couldn't create," Ari said. "Why should you be able to figure out the reasons for that in a split second? Don't you think it's going to take a little time?"

This cheered her. "Well, all right. But how will I learn?"

"Picture the thing you always wanted. What was it?"

She had the answer on the tip of her tongue. "To spin stories like Scheherazade," the ghost said with real passion. "To hold audiences captive. I knew Scheherazade. She had something I didn't have. Some spunk. Some fire. A gleam in her eye."

"No!" Ari disagreed. "She manifested something that you didn't. There's a difference. Don't you have a fire burning in you? Of course you do!"

"She was also beautiful," the ghost continued.

"That's no way to think!" Ari leaned forward. "You are brooding about the accomplishments of others. You're thinking about Scheherazade, not about you. You're making yourself into a failure by thinking about her successes. Your despair flows from your envy."

"Thank you!" the ghost said bitterly.

"You do have potential," Ari replied calmly. "You have all the genetic material you need. Just not the mental health."

"Mental health!" the ghost exclaimed. "I've been insane for hundreds of years!"

The ghost flew up out of her seat and began circling the room at breakneck speed. She seemed out of control and bent on crashing into walls and objects. But, strange to say, she had no accidents.

"You came here because you wanted to change," Ari said softly.

"Change! How can a ghost change?"

"You keep running from the obvious. You can still think. But you won't. You have retained consciousness, but you are unwilling to grow in awareness."

Tears trickled down the ghost's cheeks.

"Even a ghost can heal," Ari said, "if she can love again."

"Love?" the ghost whispered. "Have we been talking about love?" She stopped in midair. "You mean —?"

"Love yourself. If you can accomplish that, then you will begin to love others. The desire to help will well up out of that love. One day, without noticing what a tremendous trip you have taken, you will have become a muse."

A new fluttering filled the room. Then silence descended. The ghost had vanished, her disappearance accompanied by the tinkling of bells. For a moment Ari wondered if she had really visited. He sat quietly, feeling for shifts in the universe. In a while it came to him that a little more love was present in the universe, which he took to be proof of the ghost's visit and of its successful outcome.

MORAL: You can make yourself anxious in all sorts of ways. The answer is to love yourself and, out of that love and devotion, demand that you do whatever work is necessary to reduce your experience of anxiety.

Your Anxiety Mastery Menu

TWENTY-TWO TECHNIQUES FOR MASTERING ANXIETY

Let me end this lesson with the reminder with which I will end each of our lessons: you must learn and practice anxiety-management techniques if you are to master your anxiety!

Anxiety mastery requires that you actually do the work of managing and reducing your anxiety. It is not enough to have a refined sense of why and when you become anxious: you must then do something.

Most people who know they are anxious do not make enough effort to change their situation, opting instead to "white-knuckle" life, medicate themselves with antianxiety medication (which can be useful in some circumstances), or make do with alternative medicine approaches (likes teas or homeopathic remedies).

Core work requires more than this; it requires a diligent, systematic effort to find techniques that work for you, especially cognitive ones that retrain your neurons to fire differently, and to then actually employ those techniques.

Experiment with the following twenty-two anxiety-reduction strategies, learn which ones work for you, and begin to use those that work best. Please be sure to actually use the ones that work best for you! Knowing about them is not enough — you must practice them and use them. In subsequent lessons we'll look at each of these techniques in turn and examine them more closely.

1. *Existential decisiveness.* Indecisiveness about what matters, about whether you personally matter, about whether meaning resides over here or whether it resides over there, and about what constitutes the right life for you breeds anxiety. When you tackle these issues directly and become existentially decisive, you become less anxious. The first step in becoming existentially decisive is returning the control of meaning to you by asserting — and really believing — that you are in charge of the meaning in your life.

2. *Attitude choice.* You can choose to be made anxious by every new opinion you hear, or you can choose to keep your own counsel. You can choose to be overvigilant of all the changes in your environment and overconcerned about small problems, or you can shrug away such changes and problems.

You can choose to involve yourself in every controversy, or you can choose to pick your battles and maintain a serene distance from most of life's commotion. You can choose to approach life anxiously, or you can choose to approach it calmly. It is a matter of flipping an internal switch — one that you control.

3. *Personality upgrading.* The prospect of getting some bad news makes you anxious. All wound up, you lash out at your mate, eat a ton of potato chips, shut down emotionally, or drive dangerously fast. This is your personality at work. You know that most of the people around you could use a bit of a personality upgrade — well, probably the same is true for you. The more aware and the less reactive you become, the less anxious you will feel. A key anxiety-management strategy is identifying the changes you would like to make to your personality, and then making them.

4. *Improved appraising.* Incorrectly appraising situations as more important, more dangerous, or more negative than they really are raises your anxiety level. If you consider the weight of paper you use when printing out your manuscripts important, you are making yourself anxious. If you hold it as dangerous to send out your fiction without copyrighting it because you're afraid that someone will steal it, you are making yourself anxious. If you consider form rejection letters genuine indictments of your work, every form rejection letter will make you anxious. You can significantly reduce your experience of anxiety by refusing to appraise situations as more important, more dangerous, or more negative than they in fact are.

5. *Anxiety analysis.* Most people become anxious when they think about anxiety! This dynamic prevents them from analyzing their situations and understanding what triggers their anxiety and what anxiety-management tools to employ. Once you begin to think calmly about the role anxiety plays in your life, you can arrive at real solutions. You engage in this analysis straightforwardly by wondering what provokes your anxiety and where it manifests the most, by identifying how your thoughts and behaviors increase your anxiety, and by deciding which anxiety-management tools you are going to commit to practicing and learning.

6. *Lifestyle support.* Your lifestyle either supports calmness, or it doesn't. When you rush less, create fewer unnecessary pressures and stressors, get sufficient rest and exercise, eat a healthful diet, take time to relax, include love and friendship, and live in balance, you reduce your experience of anxiety. If your style is to always arrive late, to wait until the last minute to meet deadlines, and to be disorganized, you are manufacturing anxiety. How much harder will it be to deal with the creative anxiety in your life if your very lifestyle is producing its own magnum of anxiety?

7. *Behavioral changes.* What you actually do when you feel anxious makes a big difference. Playing games or watching television for hours quells anxiety but wastes vast amounts of time. Smoking cigarettes or drinking Scotch chemically quells anxiety but increases your health risks. If a ten-minute shower or a twenty-minute walk will do just as good a job of reducing your anxiety as watching another hour of golf or smoking another several cigarettes, isn't it the behavior to choose? There are many time-wasting, unhealthy, and dispiriting ways

to manage anxiety — and many efficient, healthy, and uplifting ways too. The specific tactics you use to manage anxiety matter, since some support your life purposes and others undermine them.

8. *Deep breathing.* The simplest — and a very powerful — anxiety-management technique is deep breathing. By breathing deeply (five seconds on the inhale, five seconds on the exhale), you stop your racing mind and alert your body to the fact that you wish to be calmer. Begin to incorporate deep breaths into your daily routine, especially when you think about and approach your creative work.

9. *Cognitive work.* Changing the way you think is probably the most useful and most powerful antianxiety strategy. You can do this straightforwardly by 1) noticing what you are saying to yourself; 2) disputing the self-talk that makes you anxious or does not serve you; and 3) substituting more affirmative, positive, or useful self-talk. This three-step process really works if you commit to it.

10. *Incanting.* A variation on strategies eight and nine is to use them together and to drop a useful cognition into a deep breath, thinking half the thought on the inhale and half the thought on the exhale. Incantations that might reduce your experience of anxiety are "I am perfectly calm" or "I trust my resources." Experiment with some short phrases, and find one or two that, when dropped into a deep breath, help you quell your anxious feelings.

11. *Physical relaxation techniques.* Physical relaxation techniques include such simple procedures as rubbing your shoulders and

such elaborate ones as slowly relaxing each part of your body in turn. Doing something physically soothing probably does not amount to a full anxiety-management practice but can prove really useful in the moment and when used in combination with your cognitive practice.

12. *Mindfulness techniques.* Meditation and other mindfulness practices that help you take charge of your thoughts and get a grip on your mind can prove a very useful part of your anxiety-management program. It is not as important to become a practice "sitter" or to spend long periods of time meditating as it is to truly grasp the idea that the contents of your mind create suffering and anxiety and that the more you release those thoughts and replace them with more affirmative ones, the less you will experience anxiety.

13. *Guided imagery.* Guided imagery is a technique in which you guide yourself to calmness by mentally picturing a calming image or a series of images. You might picture yourself on a blanket by the beach, walking by a lake, or swinging on a porch swing. You can use single snapshot images or combine images so that you end up with the equivalent of a short relaxation film that you can play for yourself. The first step is to determine what images actually calm you by trying out various ones. Once you've landed on images that have the right calming effect, you can bring them to mind whenever you feel anxious.

14. *Disidentification techniques and detachment training.* Disidentification is the core idea of the branch of psychotherapy known as psychosynthesis. Rather than attaching too much

significance to a passing thought, feeling, worry, or doubt, you remind yourself that you are larger than and different from all the stray, temporal events that seem so important in the moment. You do this disidentifying primarily by watching your language. For example, you stop saying, "I'm anxious" (or worse, "I'm an anxious person") and begin to say, "I'm having a passing feeling of anxiety." When your novel goes out of print, instead of saying "I'm ruined" or "I'm finished," you say, "I'm having a passing feeling of pain and disappointment." By making these linguistic changes you fundamentally reduce your experience of anxiety.

One of the best ways to reduce your anxiety is to learn to bring a calm, detached perspective to life and to turn yourself into someone whose default approach to life is to create calmness rather than drama and stress. You do this by remembering that while you can exert influence you can't control outcomes and by affirming that you are different from and larger than any component of your life: any feeling, any thought, any ruined project, any rejection — anything. By taking a more philosophical, phlegmatic, and detached approach to life (without giving up your desires, dreams, or goals) you meet life more calmly.

15. *Affirmations and prayers.* Affirmations and prayers are simply short cognitions that point your mind in the direction you want it (and you) to go. If you are feeling hatred, which breeds conflict and anxiety, you affirm your desire to love, the availability of love, or some other formulation that will reduce your experience of anxiety. By affirming your talent, your ability to trust yourself, your willingness to show up and do the work

of creating, and so on, you talk yourself into a better frame of mind and as a result feel less anxious.

16. *Ceremonies and rituals.* Creating and using a ceremony or ritual is a simple but powerful way to reduce anxiety. For many people lowering the lights, lighting candles, putting on soothing music, and in other ways ceremonially creating a calming environment helps significantly. One particularly useful ceremony is one that you create to mark the movement from "ordinary life" to "creating time." You might use an incantation like "I am completely stopping" to help you move from the rush of everyday life to the quiet of your creative work, repeating it a few times so that you actually do stop, grow quiet, and move calmly and effortlessly into the trance of working.

17. *Reorienting techniques.* If your mind starts to focus on some anxiety-producing thought or situation, or if you feel yourself becoming too wary, watchful, or vigilant, all of which are anxiety states, you can consciously turn your attention in another direction and reorient yourself away from your anxious thoughts and toward a more neutral stimulus. For example, instead of focusing on the audience entering the concert hall, which you know increases your anxiety, you might reorient yourself toward the notices on the bulletin board in the green room and casually glance at them, paying them just enough attention to take your mind off the sounds of the audience arriving but not so much attention that you lose your sense of the music you are about to play.

18. *Preparation techniques.* You can reduce your anxiety by being well prepared for anxiety-producing situations. If public speaking makes you anxious and you're about to give talks

and interviews in support of your new book, preparing answers beforehand will help with the interviews, and preparing your bookstore chat will help with the book signings. Because a great deal of the anxiety we experience is anticipatory, carefully preparing is the key to reducing this type of anxiety.

19. *Symptom confrontation techniques.* A rarely used technique, employed mostly in some forms of therapy and by some teachers in the performing arts, symptom confrontation is the idea that by "demanding" that your anxiety symptoms grow worse and worse — that your querulous singing voice or jumpy violin bowing wrist get even shakier — and by actively trying to increase your anxiety, you reach a point where you break through into laughter and a sense of the absurdity of your worries. This is a powerful technique that probably works best, however, in the context of coaching or therapy.

20. *Discharge techniques.* Anxiety and stress build up in the body, so techniques that vent that stress can prove very useful. One discharge technique that actors sometimes use to reduce their anxiety before a performance is to silently scream — to make the facial gestures and whole-body intentions that go with uttering a good cleansing scream without actually uttering any sound (which would be inappropriate in most settings). Jumping jacks, push-ups, and strong physical gestures of all sorts can be used to help release the venom of stress and anxiety and pass it out of your system.

21. *Pharmaceuticals.* Taking antianxiety medication is an option with some pluses and many minuses. The major plus is that a chemical tranquilizer, if it happens to work for you, will create an induced experience of calm. That state of calm can

provide you with a crucial respite from your anxiety and allow you to begin trying nonchemical solutions that you might not have felt equal to trying while highly anxious. Among the minuses are the side effects of chemicals, the potential for dependency, and the way they divert us from looking for better solutions.

22. *Recovery work.* You can deal with mild anxiety without having to stop everything and without making anxiety management a daily priority. But if your anxiety is more serious and especially if it permeates your life, affecting your ability to create, your ability to relate, your ability to dream large, and your very ability to live, then you must take your anxiety-management efforts very seriously, as seriously as you would take your efforts to recover from severe depression or from an addiction. One smart way to pay this kind of serious attention is by using addiction-recovery ideas, for example, the idea of identifying triggers, those thoughts and situations that trigger anxiety in you. Just as you might work your program to stay sober, you work your program to stay calm and centered.

☑ TO DO

Explore this list and learn what works for you — and truly make use of the techniques that work. Start to own at least one or two anxiety-management strategies, practice them, and make real and regular use of them. In subsequent chapters I'll describe each of these techniques in more detail, focusing on one technique per chapter.

CHAPTER 2

THE ANXIETY OF MATTERING AND NOT MATTERING

The biggest challenge facing a creative person is keeping the belief firmly in place that what she is attempting matters to her. A creative person's main challenge is therefore existential: she easily loses the sense that what she is doing matters, given how many novels or paintings there are in the world, how hard it is to do the work well, how difficult the marketplace feels, and all the rest.

Two kinds of anxiety arise with respect to this profound existential issue: the kind that arises when we begin to sense that our work doesn't matter to us and the kind that arises when we realize that our work matters very much to us (and what a burden all that mattering puts on our shoulders!). These core existential anxieties exist for every intelligent, sensitive person who has "peeked behind the curtain" and thought for herself about the nature of existence and her place in the universe.

As you work on your novel, painting, or song, accept that you will be made anxious by doubts about whether your creative efforts really matter. These doubts afflict all contemporary creative people in a way that they never afflicted indigenous potters, carvers, or weavers. The great painters at the turn of the twentieth century who fell in love with African art recognized that those tribal artists worked with a pure power because they did not doubt what they were doing. By contrast they, in avant-garde Paris, were plagued by doubts about the meaning and purpose of life.

We must accept that we have reached a point in the life of our species where enormous doubts about the nature of existence provoke persistent existential anxiety in every creative person. We deal with those doubts by announcing that it is our job to make meaning, even if the universe does not care about meaning. We embrace the profound paradigm shift from looking for and wondering about meaning to making meaning out of whole cloth and getting on with the creative work that it is in our heart to do.

HEADLINE

Anxiety arises in us when we fear that our efforts do not matter, and it arises in us when we do the creative work that matters to us. Since anxiety will arise in either case, decide to do work that matters to you, even if doing so provokes anxiety. Refuse to countenance the thought that you and your efforts do not matter — really banish that thought — and accept that when you opt to matter you will provoke anxiety that you will then have to master.

☑ TO DO

Opt to matter. This is a decision, not a given! Decide to be the hero of your own story and to prove the exception by doing your creative work, despite your doubts, anxieties, and life's difficulties. Plan for your creative work, schedule your creative work into your daily routine (preferably first thing each morning), and do it despite your doubts about you, the marketplace, and the universe.

VOW

I matter, and my creative efforts matter.

ARI TEACHING TALE

THE DANCER WHO DIDN'T MATTER

Magdalene, a dancer, came to the oasis. "I have too many interests, too many talents," she said. She had on the bluest dress, which made her eyes look wild and fierce. "First, I dance. But I also have a painter's eye. And I love to write. I've been keeping journals for years and years and have thirty fat journals filled with my thoughts. I do collages, digital photography, raku. I write songs. I want to put all this together into something, I want to figure out how to concentrate on one thing, because —" She hesitated. "The fact of the matter is, I never complete anything. I start all these incredible projects, but then something else starts to interest me more, and I begin on it. That's what's been happening..." she ended, trailing off as if her thoughts had failed her.

"The thing you want to concentrate on? What is that?"

"Well, I thought I might do a family history, maybe an oral history or a video history of my family, with my own drawings included. I've thought of doing a novel about fifteenth-century France — I've made notes about that. It would be about a young woman who stands up to the French Inquisition and is tortured and sentenced to be burned at the stake. But a young priest helps her escape. I've had the idea to do that novel for the longest time."

"You could do those things," Ari said blandly.

"I could." Magdalene fell silent. "I have so many things I want to do!" she exclaimed suddenly. "I can't seem to choose."

"No," Ari said, "it isn't quite that."

Magdalene colored. "You think I'm just avoiding —"

"No. You think that you're just avoiding choosing. I think the problem is quite different. I think you believe that nothing is worth doing, that neither you nor your efforts matter. The problem isn't that you have too many interests and talents. The problem is that you don't believe that you matter."

"That isn't true!" Magdalene cried. "I know that art matters!"

"I didn't say that. I said that you don't believe that *you* matter."

Magdalene slumped down. Ari noticed that a cool afternoon breeze had come up. He could smell the sweet jasmine tea from the tea shop a few doors down, the scent carried on the desert wind.

"When you told your parents that you wanted to be a dancer, what did they say?" Ari inquired.

"They told me to get a job and dance on the side," Magdalene replied softly.

"They told you that dancing didn't matter."

"Yes."

"When you thought about showing them your poetry, what did you think the next second?"

"That they wouldn't be interested. That they would tell me to get my real homework done."

"They told you that poetry didn't matter."

"Yes."

"When you hung things up —"

"They told me not to make holes in the wall."

"They told you that visual images didn't matter."

"Yes."

"And music —"

"They hated how much money I wanted to spend on CDs. And the kind of music! They hated that I always listened to it. They couldn't believe that I could do my homework and also listen to music, even when I brought home straight A's."

"They told you that music didn't matter."

"Yes."

"Did they believe that anything was sacred?"

"No."

"Did they believe that you were sacred?"

"No."

"Neither do you."

Magdalene's eyes welled up with tears.

"What should I do?" she asked after a long moment.

"Decide to matter. Affirm that you exist. Call yourself sacred."

The desert silence embraced them. At a corner of the oasis, near the great well encircled by fig trees, a man with one leg played a reed flute. His song drifted on the breeze and entered through the open back door.

"I always wanted to write a story about summer camp, when I had my first period," Magdalene said in a dreamy voice. "That story always felt different from the other things I wanted to do. Those other things were clever, intriguing, exciting. But this little story, it had a different feeling."

"You could see your soul in that story?"

"Yes."

"Write that story. Will it matter?"

Magdalene hesitated.

"That's the wall that confronts you, the thought you just had," Ari said. "That story has your soul in it. But the instant I asked you if it mattered, an existential doubt so huge that it swallowed up all your reasons for existing rose up like bile."

"I hate that I've been ruined this way," Magdalene whispered.

"So, the question is, Do you exist?"

Magdalene began sobbing.

"You'll write this story?" Ari continued.

"Yes," she replied between her sobs.

"If you can't, you'll call me. We'll talk."

"I'd rather come back!" Magdalene exclaimed suddenly. She sat up and brushed back her tears. "If I can't write this story I will come back and see you again."

"It's more than seven thousand miles," Ari said, but not in a way meant to discourage her.

"I know! But I matter enough to make the trip. I do exist!"

MORAL: What people say and what you encounter may reinforce your sense that you do not matter. Do not believe that false evidence!

Your Anxiety Mastery Menu

HIGHLIGHTING: EXISTENTIAL DECISIVENESS

Encountering a crouching tiger produces one sort of anxiety. Watching a cloud pass across the sun and suddenly wondering whether life is worth living produces a very different sort. Thoughts of the latter kind — Do I matter? Do my creative efforts matter? Why bother trying if I'm only here for a handful of years? Why fight off my baser impulses and my shadows if nothing arbitrates morality? and so on — produce that modern anxiety that existential writers have been describing for a century. It is an anxiety that no thoughtful, sensitive contemporary person can fully escape.

Yet while you can't escape it, you can minimize it. You can become more decisive about what matters; about whether you personally matter; about where, how, when, and why to invest meaning; and about what constitutes the right life for you. You can become more existentially decisive. The first step is returning control of meaning to you by asserting — and really believing — that you are in charge of your life's meaning. Once you fully grasp that meaning is a subjective psychological experience and that you have the final say on your subjective experiences, you have a way of instantly responding to every passing existential cloud.

This change sounds like the following. Instead of letting that cloud passing in front of the sun provoke existential anxiety, you say to yourself, "Nope, not interested. I know exactly where meaning resides — in me — and I know exactly what I'm doing with my life. I'm not buying any angst, worry, dread, or anything dark and cold today. Nope. I refuse to let this cloud be a meaning crisis and a way to let me off the hook from making meaning today. I could certainly let the anxiety in, start drinking, and lose this week, but I know better, and I'm simply not interested in letting this tiny existential incident precipitate a crisis of doubt."

Of course, that is a very wordy response, and you'll want to shorten it in real life! In fact, you want it to be a stance and not a matter of words. You want to stand tall, existentially speaking, and become someone who has answered all the ultimate questions with this ultimate answer, that while you are on earth in the human form of a squat writer or a sinuous dancer you will live a principled, value-driven, creative, ballsy life full of as much joy as you can stand and as much effort as you can muster — and that's that. You do not allow any cloud passing in front of the sun to affect you, because the doubts about existence lurking in those shadows are not your doubts. You no longer harbor those doubts.

Well, you say, maybe on ordinary days I can pull that off, but what about on really taxing days, existentially speaking?

Aren't those doubts destined to return by virtue of the very nature of existence? Can I stay existentially decisive on the day I get a cancer diagnosis or lose a loved one in a car accident? Isn't life infinitely able to remind me that, in the cosmic scheme of things, I don't really matter, all my affirmations and efforts notwithstanding? Well, yes, it is. It can knock anyone off his or her high existential horse. But you can factor life's power to devalue and diminish you into your everyday heroic stance.

You do this by internally saying the following: "I am going to do my darnedest to make personal meaning by investing meaning in my art, in loving and being loved, in ethical action, in all sorts of meaning opportunities, in dozens and scores of meaning opportunities, even as I know full well that the facts of existence can knock me down at any moment with a really painful toothache or worse — much worse. I am going to remain as existentially decisive as I can, starting out each day making conscious meaning investments and living according to my purposes, even as I hold in a corner of consciousness the undeniable knowledge that while I am the captain of my soul, I am not the master of my fate. I can only do what I can do — but I will do that!"

Again, this is a lot to say! You want to feel this without having to say all these words. You want to genuinely, deeply, truly feel this. You want to feel it even if you are stuck with a dreary day job, a half-finished novel you hate, and few prospects. You want to feel it even if you have just broken up with your lover and mice have invaded your studio. You want to feel existentially decisive even if the game is not going well. If you decide unequivocally and irrevocably that you matter, you will have only your day job, novel, prospects, love life, and mice to deal with — you won't also have to deal with the anxiety of existential doubt. This one less thing is a mountain of a thing not to have looming up as, at three in the morning, you turn over in bed and get a whiff of nothingness. Existentially decisive, certain that you are going to live for all intents and purposes as if you matter, you calmly fall right back asleep.

☑ TO DO

Describe in your own words what becoming existentially decisive means to you.

CHAPTER 3

THE ANXIETY OF IDENTITY

Once we begin to really fall in love with a creative discipline, we begin the process of identity formation and begin to call ourselves a writer, painter, filmmaker, musician, singer, actor, and so on. As this process unfolds, we begin to add more and more pieces to this identity, sometimes for good reasons and sometimes not. We may add "heavy drinking" and "don't need anybody!" to our Ernest Hemingway version of our writer identity or "manic-depressive" and "highly sensitive" to our Virginia Woolf version of our writer identity, not so much because we are those things but because we somehow think that they belong to a writer's identity.

In this unconscious fashion our identity begins to build — and makes us anxious because we understand in a corner of our consciousness that we are not really that persona we have adopted. At the same time we may have trouble growing into the identity we actually need to nurture, the one that includes personality traits such as discipline, self-direction, self-trust, resiliency, flexibility, concentration, and spontaneity. On the one hand, we build a false self that is made up of cultural constructs and bits of romanticism, and on the other we fail to construct an authentic self that might actually be equal to the rigors of the creative life. This secret knowledge, tucked away in a corner of awareness, that we have not created ourselves in our best image, haunts us and provokes anxiety.

It is never too late to do the sort of personality analysis and personality work that will help you grow into the person you would like to be. This personality work involves identifying false bits of personality to eliminate and desired personality traits to nurture. If you have serious problems, say, with an addiction to alcohol or cocaine, you will need to do full-scale recovery work. Personality work is possible — countless addicts in recovery can attest to that reality — but it is real work that will require your complete attention. Similarly, adding wanted traits like discipline or concentration won't happen overnight or without a struggle. But if you can manage this heroic work, you will become your real self and, in the process, reduce a substantial amount of your anxiety.

HEADLINE

When your sense of who you are does not match your sense of who you ought to be, you experience anxiety. Become the person you long to see in the mirror, and match your reality to your vision of your authentic self.

☑ TO DO

Actively become your best version of yourself by working on your personality. Begin by identifying the traits and qualities you want to shed and the traits and qualities you want to nurture. Choose one from each list, and make a plan for eliminating the one and increasing the other.

VOW

I will strip away all the personality bits that are not me, add the traits that I need, and create and stand behind my authentic self.

ARI TEACHING TALE

THE FAMILY OF FRUSTRATED ARTISTS

The sky was azure, and the bazaar hummed with activity. Ari left the shop between clients to purchase some dates for himself and his daughter, Maya. At the last minute he decided to purchase some extra dates to share with his next client, a poet from the bayou country of Louisiana.

When he returned he presented Maya with her dates and put the rest on a plate that he set out on the table between two upholstered armchairs. A moment later the poet appeared.

"I believe your books have saved my life," she began, once she was seated. She was dressed genteelly but looked to have suffered a lot. "I really believed that I was going crazy. Now I realize that the only thing that has helped me want to live, that has stopped me from going crazy, and that pulled me through the really rough times, was creativity. My artistic yearnings saved me. I am learning to trust them and to believe that they are a gift from God.

"I think that I've always been an artist," she continued, smoothing out her dress, "and now I believe that most of the people in my family were artists too. Unfortunately, they've all been blocked artists. I think that the worst family situation is a family of blocked artists. My family has been marred by alcoholism and violence. I believe that these conditions have existed because they never knew that it was safe to be an artist. It seemed when I tried to be an artist, I always had to do or be something else. And being that something else always took me away from my art, my love. I had to learn that if I practice my art that doesn't make me odd or weird. I was never willing to see that until I read your books.

"I discovered something else. Since I did not know that it was safe to be an artist, I tried my best to punish myself for trying. It's as if I thought that being an artist was a bad thing. At least, that was how I was taught. It was not a readily identifiable lesson, but it was there all the time. I've discovered that there are a thousand ways to kill myself. The easiest are gunshots, overdoses, and razors. The ones I chose were being in violent relationships, forsaking needed dental and medical care, dabbling in a humiliating alcohol addiction, and wallowing in deep depression and fear. It's funny that people never mention those as attempts at suicide. They are, but they take a little bit longer."

Ari nodded. "Date?" he said, holding out the plate.

"No, thank you. I can't eat anything that sweet. My teeth."

Ari took a date for himself and put the plate back on the table.

"So," she continued, "I was told not to think. I was told not to feel. I was told to follow, not lead. I was told that the world was filled with sin, devils, Jews, Mexicans, whores, artists. I was not taken to exhibitions of modern art or even to the library. No one had to tell me directly that art was evil. I had my schoolgirl drawings put up on the refrigerator. I wrote a story in third grade that my family admired. I even went to dance lessons for a while. But all that meant nothing. The real message was, 'Like us, you do not count, and you will not amount to anything.' No one had to tell me directly not to be an artist. My whole upbringing did that, my family did that, my world did that, and the very look of the furniture in my living room screamed it. Place: low. Possibilities: none. Art: never.

"But," she said, "despite all that, I know that my family was a family of artists. Does that make sense? Does that seem possible?"

"Yes," Ari replied. "Absolutely. I know exactly what you mean."

"So I did careless, self-defacing things," the poet resumed. "My brothers, on the other hand, were violent. They were filled with rage and hate. They hated women who accomplished anything, and they hated men who accomplished anything — unless they were bullies and sadists, like certain high school coaches. They were ruined, and they knew it. But they were also artists.

Frustrated artists. Men who were born with a chance, who had the seed of God in them, but who turned into monsters. We could have been beautiful, but we didn't make it."

"Tea?" Ari said. "I have some black tea with spices that tastes sweet but won't hurt your teeth."

"That would be very nice," the poet said, smiling.

MORAL: You may start to be separated from your authentic self from the very moment of birth. Notice that separation! — and start your journey home.

Your Anxiety Mastery Menu

HIGHLIGHTING: ATTITUDE CHOICE

If you believe that your attitude is outside your control, in whose control do you believe it to be? Do you believe that you *must* be pessimistic because you have plenty of reasons for being so? Do you take it that you *must* be depressed because so many things are going miserably? Do you believe that you *must* keep a wary, critical eye on every aspect of your environment because you were harmed as a child and felt unsafe and unloved? You might well respond, "Well, I just don't have any reason to feel sunny, phlegmatic, and philosophical about life because life tends to suck," to which I must respond, "That's a mistake, and a sure road to anxiety."

It turns out that a pessimistic, self-critical, world-wary, half-depressed, passive, defeated attitude, even if you can produce a ton of reasons why that is the logical attitude to adopt, does not feel good, does not serve you, and is bound to make you anxious. Even if you can produce a mountain of evidence for why you ought to feel gloomy, wary, and out of sorts, it doesn't follow that actually being gloomy, wary, and out of sorts is the way for you to be. You will have to decide two things if you want to reduce your experience of anxiety and put yourself in a position to create regularly and live well: that your attitude is in your control and that you intend to adopt an attitude that serves you.

What is that right attitude? First of all, one that is less anxiously vigilant. You can choose to be overvigilant to changes in your environment and overconcerned with small problems, or you can shrug off such changes and problems. Second, one that is more assured. Opt for confidence — not bravado, not arrogance, not grandiosity, but confidence — and decide to believe in yourself, your path, your inner resources, your choices, and your ability to right your ship if it drifts off course. Third, one that is more self-directing. You can choose to involve yourself in every controversy and keep abreast of every story, or you can choose to maintain a serene distance from most of life's commotion. Becoming less vigilant, more confident, more self-directing. that's a start!

The most basic change to make is to approach life less anxiously. You would think that would go without saying! Yet it is as much your anxious attitude that makes you anxious as it is anything else. That is the mother of all attitude changes, giving yourself the gift of everyday calmness. You believe in yourself more, you worry less, you keep your own counsel, you stay existentially decisive, you shrug more and frown less. You can choose to approach life this way, or you can choose to approach it timidly, nervously, and anxiously. It is a matter of flipping an internal switch — one that you control.

Where is this switch? A brain scan won't show it. You won't find a dollar-off coupon for it in the Sunday paper. It isn't at the end of a vision quest hidden behind a sand dune in a faraway desert. It is simply the mind concluding something. It is an alcoholic extricating himself from his third car crash and saying, "Okay. Enough." It is the mind changing its mind. It is billions of neurons reorganizing themselves in the blink of an eye and delivering a new, somber message of hope. It is you deciding.

☑ TO DO

Flipping the switch is only the first step. Then you must live your attitude change. You must begin to carefully not notice the small things that previously made you anxious; or, if you do notice them, you must breathe, smile, and let their threat pass instantly. You must live your attitude change in the vortex of exactly those things that have always made you anxious. Do I need to say that this is real work? But the reward is calmness. Flip the switch. Change your attitude. Live the change.

CHAPTER 4

THE ANXIETY OF INDIVIDUALITY

Creativity is an expression of individuality, an expression of a person's desire to manifest her potential, to speak in her own voice, to have her own opinions, and to do her own work. What distinguishes the creative person from other people is her felt sense of individuality. Many people are born conventional and find it easy to follow the crowd; only some people are born with a strong desire to assert their individuality. All the personality traits that creative people manifest, from a risk-taking orientation to a need for solitude — the more than seventy-five traits that have been described in the creativity literature — flow from this single core quality: the need to assert individuality.

A person born individual will, within a few years of her birth, feel that difference as she looks around her and is unable to understand why the people she sees are acting so conventionally. As a result she is likely to feel alienated, out of place, like a stranger in a strange land. Even if she trains herself to hold her tongue and engage in conventional work, an individual of this sort will already know as a young child that she can't really conform and that she wasn't built to conform. To call this budding creator a nonconformist is only to call her an individual. They are different ways of saying the same thing.

With this felt sense of individuality comes anxiety. The sources of this anxiety are several. First, she experiences a special sense of responsibility — she is responsible to herself and responsible for maintaining her ideals, manifesting her potential, and making herself proud — and this sense of responsibility provokes anxiety as she feels a persistent pressure to meet her expectations for herself. Second, she must continually battle her conventional peers for her right to be individual, which provokes anxiety. She is made anxious trying to meet her own standards, and she is made anxious fighting off the fit-in-and-make-nice demands of conventional society.

The answer? It isn't that you must become conventional! — but rather that you must learn to effectively deal with the anxiety of individuality. Nature has created a person who must know for herself, follow her own path, and be herself, has put it in her mind that she was born to do special work, and then turns around and plagues her with anxiety. Well, so be it. At least nature has also provided you with some anxiety-management tools!

HEADLINE

The struggle to become and remain the individual you were born to be creates every manner of anxiety. The answer isn't to surrender to conventionality but to master the anxiety of individuality.

✓ TO DO

Analyze how individuality and anxiety are connected in your life. I've provided you with some headlines, but each person's reality is more complex and dynamic than can be captured in a few phrases. For you, the issue may be your inability to become the individual you wanted to become and the anxiety generated by having fallen short of your expectations. Or the issue may be entirely different — maybe you've been able to retain your individuality but at some very high costs, costs that bring with them their own special brand of anxiety. Take some time and carefully analyze your situation.

VOW

I must be myself. That will provoke anxiety, and I will deal with it.

PHOEBE TEACHING TALE

The following teaching tale features Phoebe, a precocious girl of thirteen who's begun to write her first novel. Like the Ari teaching tales, this one employs naturalistic and fantastic elements and presents a moral in fictional form. Enjoy!

THE BOY WHO BURIED HIS INVENTION

Phoebe trudged off to school early one Monday morning. As she passed the park, she saw a figure digging in the dirt between two tall pines. She was about to hurry on when she recognized Albert, the strangest student at Lincoln Middle School. Albert was a brilliant eighth-grader who marched so entirely to his own drummer that he'd been exempted from many of Lincoln's basic procedures. For instance, he took math classes at the junior college, not at Lincoln, and was set to go to college straight from middle school.

Phoebe had heard a trillion stories about Albert, some of which had to be true. Supposedly he worked in a lab behind his parents' house, had written articles on molecular biology that had appeared in reviewed journals, was friends with famous scientists at Berkeley, Stanford, and Cal Tech, and had presented at some international conferences. He also had sad eyes, a stooped walk, and looked every bit the tortured genius. Here was Albert now, apparently burying something in the ground.

Phoebe entered the park and joined him beside the hole he'd dug. Albert stopped what he was doing, nodded, and resumed filling the hole. After a moment he put down his spade.

"Do you know who Nikolai Tesla was?" he asked.

"Yes!" she replied. "I do." Phoebe was proud of her breadth of knowledge. "He was an eccentric inventor who came up with the Tesla coil, whatever that is, and lots of other things. He liked to walk the streets of New York City late at night carrying bread crumbs for the pigeons. Then there was the famous incident with the reporters."

"You know about that too?"

Suddenly Phoebe realized what was going on here. A chill ran down her spine.

"Yes. Tesla claimed to have invented a death ray," Phoebe continued, eying Albert's burial site. "Today people hypothesize that it might have been a laser. He invited reporters to see his death ray in action. He demonstrated it and then destroyed it in their presence. He said that people would only use his invention to wage war on each other, and he wouldn't have it. The story may be apocryphal, though whether or not his demonstration really took place should be simple to decide. I mean, either all those reporters showed up, or they didn't!" Phoebe caught her breath. "Is this something like that?"

"Yes." He finished filling the hole. "A few days ago I invented a device that can aerosol any naturally occurring compound. It was incredibly simple to do. The main problem with biological weapons is getting them into aerosol shape. I've taken care of that."

A second chill ran down Phoebe's spine.

"Why — ?"

"I wasn't playing with biological weapons. I was interested in nanotechnology and its interface with chaos theory. I was curious about the turbulence of molecules. One thing led to another."

"Golly," Phoebe said.

"I know that somebody will figure this out. For all I know they've figured it out already. But that's neither here nor there. I am going to take responsibility for my own inventing. What I know gets buried here."

"It —" Phoebe hesitated. "If this were 1944 —"

"I know! Would I have worked on the Manhattan Project? I don't know. Should I give this to our military, since our military is the tool of a government that's better than most? I'm really not sure. That strikes me as a very reasonable argument. Still, I feel compelled to keep this technology secret. I could be wrong. Very wrong. But that's what I've decided."

Phoebe nodded. "This is a lot harder than choosing which short story to write! You know, my mom is a bioethicist. She has to think along these lines and make these kinds of decisions. Would you like to talk to her?" Phoebe paused. "I know you've made your decision already. But I wonder if you might want to chat about it."

That evening they gathered in the Barlow living room. Albert explained his situation, and Phoebe's parents understood instantly.

"I think you've analyzed it perfectly," Phoebe's mom said.

"So you think I was right to bury it?" Albert asked.

"That's not quite the same question," Phoebe's mom replied. "I think you're quite right to presume that your invention would end up in the hands of the military and be used to produce weapons that in all likelihood would eventually kill people. Those are the likely facts. The question remains, What is the right thing to do? What does 'the right thing to do' even mean?

Historically, only easy answers have been offered. The Platonic ideal is to try to match your situation against the ideal of right thing to do and see if it matches. But no one knows what that ideal is, so that process entirely begs the question. The Aristotelian ideal is to use reason, which also leads nowhere in particular, since no amount of pure reason could ever help you determine what ethical principle, if any, was higher than any other ethical principle. No amount of pure reason could really help you predict the outcome of such a complex set of circumstances or even help you nail down what 'ethical principle' might mean. The existential ideal is to look human nature in the eye and accept that one burden of freedom is the responsibility to choose. But nothing in that formula helps you know what's right to choose and what's wrong. As to religious thought, well, believers are never asked to think hard about anything. The whole of intellectual history gives you next to nothing to go on, which is why each person who feels obliged to act ethically one day finds himself facing this blank wall."

Albert shook his head. "So how do you make your bioethical decisions?"

"First of all, to call them 'ethical' is something of a stretch. They are more 'utilitarian with a nod to fairness' than 'ethical.' Someone draws up the guidelines. Usually it's a committee made up of different constituencies — doctors, lawyers, professors, businesspeople, politicians — all with different agendas and a different sense of right and wrong. Then we try to apply those guidelines in individual cases. And decide when and if an exception might be in order."

"All that begs the same questions," Albert murmured.

"That's right, Albert."

Albert shook his head. Everyone waited.

"Is this a good country?" he asked after a bit.

"The best," Phoebe's dad answered. "Although we also do a ton of miserable, cruel, and unethical things."

"That doesn't help me decide."

"I know."

Phoebe sat up. "A clerk at the International Crafts Shop explained the difference between deontology and teleology to me," she began. "She went on to say that neither really works. You can't say that the means are more important than the end or that the end justifies the means. What she uses for herself is what she calls 'my ethics' — that is, her own ethics. I think that's the only sensible way. The best we can do is to try to take a lot into account, as much as our brain can handle, and then somehow decide what's right."

"Somehow or other," Albert said. "Is that all there is?"

"Yes, I'm afraid so," said Phoebe's mother.

"Yes, that's about it," said Phoebe's father.

"Would you like a Pink Lemonade Snapple?" Phoebe inquired. "That always helps me."

"No, thank you." Albert got to his feet. Hunched over, he looked ancient for a boy. "I'm just not sure. It feels safer keeping my technology buried than turning it over to the Pentagon. But is 'safer' the same as 'right'? I don't know. I guess...I guess I'll sleep on it."

"Come back any time," Phoebe's mom said. "We can have tuna fish sandwiches."

"Unless the issue of tuna harvesting is a moral quagmire and we take to eating weeds," said Phoebe's dad.

"Though 'weed' is merely pejorative and not suitable for anybody's moral philosophy," Phoebe countered.

They all laughed. Even Albert. But his eyes weren't smiling. He had created something amazing and terrible, and now he had to reckon with what he had wrought.

MORAL: You are the arbiter of everything — and, yes, that will provoke some anxiety.

Your Anxiety Mastery Menu

HIGHLIGHTING: PERSONALITY UPGRADING

Personality is both formed and fluid, static and dynamic. If the brain is the most complex bit of matter in the universe, personality may amount to the most complex set of dynamics in the universe. Sometimes you react reflexively; sometimes you stop yourself from acting reflexively and consider your reaction. Sometimes you operate from the shadows, leading with the dark side of your personality; sometimes you operate from the light. Sometimes you feel yourself to be nothing but a walking addiction; sometimes you act in a principled and disciplined way for days on end. You — we — are exactly this mass of contradictions.

Nevertheless, we are obliged to figure ourselves out and

make any changes that we deem necessary. In working with therapy clients, creativity coaching clients, and meaning coaching clients for more than twenty years, I've found that perhaps the most useful tool for self-exploration is writing an autobiography from twelve to fifteen pages long. If you do that writing, you are almost certain to learn a great deal about who you are. Focus on going deep and being real, not on beautiful memoir writing. Try to arrive at a sense of what motivates you, what subverts you, and why you react in the idiosyncratic ways you do.

If you are brave enough to appraise your personality and arrive at some conclusions about what changes you want to make, you will still be faced with the enormous challenge of actually changing your personality. To do so, you must take three steps: you must state a clear goal with nameable behaviors, you must practice those behaviors in your mind's eye, and you must adopt those behaviors in real-life situations. For example, you might name as a goal "becoming more assertive." Then you name the behaviors that go with that goal, for example, "the next time Jim criticizes me, I will tell him to stop." Next you rehearse in your mind's eye. Finally, when Jim does criticize you, even though you don't feel even slightly up to the task, you manage to tell him to stop.

It is splendid to act assertively when we have decided that we want to become more assertive. But if it is our style to be meek, then a single assertive response will not do the trick. We need to repeat our desired behaviors over and over, forgive ourselves when we slip and react too meekly, continue practicing and rehearsing, and pay attention to our goals every day. We stay focused on our intentions, cherish our successes, and remain mindful of the fact that slips remain a persistent possibility. If you can upgrade your personality in this way, identifying the changes you want to make and then making them, you will significantly reduce your experience of anxiety.

☑ TO DO

Appraise your personality for strengths and weaknesses. Start working today on the weaknesses.

CHAPTER 5

THE ANXIETY OF CHOOSING
THE CREATIVE LIFE

What could be more natural than wanting to create? There is an enormous leap to be made, however, from taking deep pleasure in writing a lovely paragraph to announcing that you intend to be a short story writer. That is a leap over a roiling, sulfurous river of easy-to-anticipate difficulties. How will you earn a living? Who, if anyone, will be interested in your stories? Will it be fair to your future family, if you have one, to have picked a path with zero real-world prospects?

Is it even the right choice for you, given that you haven't tried your hand at anything else and might actually love something different, something with prospects that short-story writing doesn't offer? Is it any wonder that anticipating that leap makes you more than a little queasy? Or that you feel hardly any better on the other side, having made the choice and run full speed into the difficulties you anticipated?

In some other culture and in some other time it might have been easy to choose what today we would call a creative life. It might have been something like second nature, culturally sanctioned and approved, to hunt in the afternoon and do some cave painting in the evening. Today you are obliged either to dabble, which tends not to feel satisfying or momentous enough, or to choose a discipline, with all the difficulties that entails. In our contemporary world, fear for the future comes with that first glimmer of creativity. Fear for the future — and anxiety.

HEADLINE

Choosing the creative life may be precisely the right thing for you to do. But it is not an innocent choice: expect anxiety.

☑ TO DO

If you have chosen the creative life, take a deep breath and accept the consequences of that choice.

VOW

If I choose the creative life, I accept that I am opening the door wide for anxieties that I might not have encountered if I had chosen some other kind of life.

PHOEBE TEACHING TALE

ELOISE'S PIANO

One Monday after school Phoebe spent a delicious hour thinking about her novel, and another sweet bit of time wondering if she might not prefer becoming a painter. Then she decided that she had better get on with her homework. But by that time she had completely run out of Pink Lemonade Snapple, which meant that there was no way she could deal with math or science. She would simply have to make a trip to the market.

She walked slowly, since there was nothing about her homework that made her want to rush back home. She turned onto Almond Lane and trudged toward her friend Eloise's house, a cozy gingerbread that sported the best decorations at Halloween, including, last year, several motorized bats. As she drew nearer, she saw Eloise sitting on the top step. She was crying. Phoebe came down the cement path and sat next to her friend.

"What's the matter?" she asked.

"It's my piano," Eloise replied. "It's gone."

"You mean someone stole it?" In her mind's eye she pictured Laurel and Hardy as the thieves, because of that old silent film that featured them as piano movers.

"No. My parents got rid of it."

"Why?" Again an inadvertent image came to mind. Phoebe had once read a short story about a poor Russian family chopping up their furniture for firewood during a fierce Siberian winter. Now she saw Eloise's parents going at their upright with axes.

"They said I played it too much. They said they were worried about me. They took the day off from work today, and when I got home from school the piano was gone."

"But you were getting your homework done?"

"Yes."

"And getting good grades? I know you were."

"The best. They even put one of those stupid bumper stickers on their car. You know, 'My child is an honor student at Abraham Lincoln Middle School.'"

"Ugh!" Phoebe agreed. "So...why did they do it?"

"I don't know."

Eloise began sobbing. Phoebe put her arm around her friend's shoulder and tried to comfort her.

"Did they warn you? Have they been on you about playing the piano?"

"They warned me, I guess. But it never made any sense. 'Eloise, stop playing the piano!' 'Eloise, you're playing the piano too much!' 'Eloise, can't you find something else to do?' Stuff like that. But...I just didn't get it."

"Are they music phobic?"

"They love music! There's always music in our house."

Phoebe shook her head. It made no sense.

They sat without speaking. A bluebird descended, pecked around a bit, and then flew off to the top branch of a tall pine. A squirrel darted along the top of the fence. At their feet, on the warm concrete, a small lizard sat sunning himself in the last rays of afternoon.

"Should I speak to them?" Phoebe asked.

"You know parents. Once they've made up their minds…"

"I know. But a piano is a terrible thing to lose!"

Eloise nodded. After another minute they got up and went into the house. The aroma of pot roast filled the hall. Phoebe knew that this was a kind family, a good home, a place where you would never yell about the piano being played. Why on earth had they done this drastic thing?

The Sylvesters were in the kitchen. Mrs. Sylvester was at the stove, stirring vegetables. Mr. Sylvester was at the kitchen table, making a salad.

"Hello, Mr. and Mrs. Sylvester," Phoebe said. "Smells good in here!"

"Hello, Phoebe," Mr. Sylvester said. "Care to stay for dinner?"

"No, thank you," Phoebe replied. "I have science homework to do. And math. Actually, I'm here on a…" She searched for the right phrase. "A mission of mercy," she said.

"What's that?" Mrs. Sylvester said.

"This is very delicate," Phoebe replied. "I don't want you to get more upset than you already are. But you need to know that Eloise misses her piano terribly, that she's heartbroken. Actually, she doesn't understand why you got rid of it in the first place."

Phoebe waited. Eloise shrunk back. Mrs. Sylvester

stopping stirring the vegetables. Mr. Sylvester stopped slicing mushrooms.

"She was playing it so much," Mrs. Sylvester said softly.

"All the time," Mr. Sylvester echoed sorrowfully.

The girls waited. No one spoke. The vegetables sizzled. Mrs. Sylvester gave them a perfunctory stir and lowered the heat under the skillet. After another long moment she addressed Phoebe.

"She might have decided to become a pianist," she whispered. "The way she was playing so much."

"She might have wanted a career as a concert soloist," Mr. Sylvester continued. "In cutthroat competition with a thousand other pianists."

"For a handful of solo possibilities," Mrs. Sylvester said.

"All the politics," Mr. Sylvester said.

"She might have ended up in a piano bar," Mrs. Sylvester murmured, her lower lip quivering. "When she might have had a much better life."

This was the horror that had caused the Sylvesters to get rid of Eloise's piano! They were deathly afraid that Eloise might become a musician. A new vision of a life in the arts, as something dreadful and threatening, wormed its way into Phoebe's consciousness.

"But you love music!" Phoebe exclaimed, recoiling at the vision.

Tears sprang to Mrs. Sylvester's eyes. "We *do* love music. That's why we know we're to blame. We know we did this to Eloise. Oh, Eloise, it isn't your fault! We turned you into a musician!"

Eloise burst out laughing. Astonished, everyone turned in Eloise's direction.

"But I don't want to be a musician!" Eloise exclaimed. "I want to be an astronaut."

"An astronaut?" Mrs. Sylvester said.

"An astronaut?" Mr. Sylvester said.

"An *astronaut*?" Phoebe said.

"Absolutely! I want to go to the Air Force Academy, become a jet pilot, enter the space program, and eventually live on a space station."

"The Air Force Academy?" Mrs. Sylvester said.

"A jet pilot?" Mr. Sylvester said.

"Enter the space program?" Mrs. Sylvester said.

"*Live on a space station?*" Phoebe said.

"Yes!" Eloise replied. "Haven't you been listening to me? About space camp? How many times have I pestered you about my wanting to go to space camp? About flying lessons? About glider lessons? About parachute jumping? Is anyone listening?"

"We just heard you playing the piano," Mrs. Sylvester said.

"All the time," Mr. Sylvester said.

"*Parachute jumping?*" Phoebe said.

"Well, there you go!" Eloise chortled. "I love playing the piano, but, seriously, can you see a piano on a space station? Do you know how much fuel you need to get a pound of stuff into space? They would *never* put a piano on a space station. Right, Phoebe?"

Phoebe agreed. The Sylvesters looked purple. A moment later they exchanged glances. Mr. Sylvester nodded, marched to the phone, and dialed a number.

"Mr. Hester?" he said. "We'd like our piano back." There was a moment's pause. "Yes, I know! A piano's not something you toss around lightly. Of course we'll pay to get it back. We need that piano!"

"Parents," Eloise said.

Phoebe shook her head.

"We could *see* you as a musician," Mrs. Sylvester said suddenly. "Because we could see *ourselves* as musicians. But we never saw you as a pilot! That never registered."

Phoebe had a thought. She turned to her friend's parents. "So you'll support Eloise in her quest to become an astronaut?" she said. "Or — I don't know — are you going to hide her parachute?"

Mr. Sylvester sighed. "We'll have to think about this."

Phoebe shook her head. "This is very important," she thought to herself. "Because one day I'm going to spring something like this on *my* parents. I'd better be ready for *their* reaction. Who knew?"

Worst of all, she wanted the pot roast. But she said her good-byes and went off in search of Pink Lemonade Snapple, without which her homework would remain undone for all eternity.

MORAL: Maybe the thought of choosing the creative life doesn't make you particularly anxious. But what if it makes everyone *around* you anxious?

Your Anxiety Mastery Menu

Highlighting: Improved Appraising

Incorrectly appraising situations as more important, more dangerous, or more negative than they in fact are raises your anxiety level. If you consider it important what weight of paper you use in printing out your manuscripts, you are making yourself anxious. If you hold it as dangerous to send out your fiction without copyrighting it because you're afraid that someone will steal it, you are making yourself anxious. If you consider form rejection letters genuine indictments of your work, every form rejection letter will make you anxious. You can significantly reduce your experience of anxiety by refusing to appraise situations as more important, more dangerous, or more negative than they really are.

The first step is to remember that *you* get to do the appraising. Life does not come with built-in threat levels. A concert before ten thousand people isn't automatically a 10 on some threat meter. It is exactly as safe or as dangerous as you feel it to be. Once you get a firm grip on the idea that you get to decide whether or not a situation is dangerous, you gain wonderful control of your anxiety. The key question is, "Is this really dangerous?" or some variation such as, "Is it really such a problem that I don't know the ending of my novel yet?" or, "Does it really seem so scary that a collector is visiting my studio?" It is the *really* in each of those questions that alerts you to the truth of the matter. Maybe it is a small problem, a little dangerous, or mildly scary — but to raise the threat level beyond that is to engage in self-sabotage.

The second step is to actually do the appraising. Do not let your mind move from some casual thought to the creation of fright without intervening and asking yourself, "What is the actual threat level here?" Imagine that you are opening your painting studio to visitors as part of your city's open studio weekend and that thinking about it is raising your anxiety level tremendously. Do not simply accept that "open studios make me anxious." Understand why they make you anxious and appraise whether your reasons amount to good ones. You may discover that four reasons stand out: that you hate to make small talk about your paintings, that you can't decide whether or not to frame your work, that you can't decide whether to serve cookies or something more substantial, and that you are scared that if no one buys anything your year will feel like a failure.

Having analyzed the situation, you can then think which of these, if any, constitute genuine threats. Probably the matter of cookies can be dispensed with pretty quickly: you just make a decision. The same with the small talk: how threatening is it really to be "forced" to make small talk? Prepare a few pat lines ("I tend only to paint on cloudy days just before the full moon") and relax. The framing is a harder one, since that involves real dollars and a real threat to your budget. There you will have to breathe, calculate, and make a decision — if you are strapped for money, almost certainly in the direction of not framing. If you hear yourself saying, "But then no one will buy anything," shake your head and exclaim, "I don't know that!" Once you decide not to frame, opt for optimism.

As to the fourth, the one that is the genuine threat — that you are banking so much on this open studio weekend that if nothing sells you will probably sink into a depression — this one you must deal with in more than a glancing way. This is the deep threat, the real threat, the one that is generating all the anxiety. You deal with it by having a frank conversation with yourself and abiding by your conclusions. This might sound like, "I can't put all my selling eggs into the basket of one open studio weekend a year. That puts too much pressure on that weekend and just isn't a smart idea. I must market in a ton of additional ways — and if I do, then this upcoming weekend won't feel like such a threat; it will feel like just one of my efforts." You conclude that you will market in lots of new ways, reducing the pressure you've put on open studio weekend and eliminating a significant portion of your anxiety.

This is the work of accurately appraising. You examine situations, you analyze them, and you decide if your initial feelings of anxiety are really warranted. Nine times out of ten you will see that they are not, that they are about as threatening as having to decide whether to serve cookies or finger sandwiches. That tenth time you will discern that the threat is genuine, that a real career mishap or depression is looming if x does or doesn't happen. For this tenth, you marshal all your resources and try to find good answers. Who else can do this essential work but you?

☑ TO DO

Change your mind about the threat level of things. If you are used to warning bells going off all the time, change their setting and rig them to go off only when the threat is real and significant.

CHAPTER 6

THE ANXIETY OF SURVIVING

f you have an independent income, that can produce its own psychological effects, but at least you do not have to worry about paying the rent or buying groceries as you attempt to write your novel or become known as a musician. If you don't have an independent income, then you have survival needs that inevitably make you anxious.

If you grow dependent on a working mate who lets you know that you are not sufficiently contributing to the family income, that makes you anxious. If you work a day job that you hate, that will make you anxious. If you are eking out a tiny living but know that you are just one commission or one series of articles away from not being able to pay the rent, that makes you anxious. If you've chosen a safe, sensible "uncreative" profession, which in fact may turn out to be neither safe nor sensible, that will make you anxious. It is a stark fact that having to pay the rent and put food on the table (not to mention providing yourself with "luxuries" like health insurance) provokes core anxiety.

Many if not most creative people spend their whole lives struggling to construct a way of living that addresses both their survival and their creative needs. Even if they manage to make enough money from their creative efforts to survive, they often find themselves disturbed by the smallness of their income, such that they can't have niceties or even a lot of necessities, and the insecurity of their income, such that ideas like retiring one day look to be out of the question. No contemporary first-world culture is set up to provide for a creative person the way that a tribal society naturally provides for its weavers, potters, and music makers, whose work is integral to tribal life. We have the rat race — and anxiety.

There is clearly no simple answer to this dilemma, which is yet another reason that you must learn to manage your anxiety. The anxiety is coming; it will accompany you as you try to address your survival needs, which may be literally most of the time. If you are lucky enough to have satisfactorily met your survival needs, perhaps because you've become successful and secure as an artist, because you have a day job that you like and that allows you time to create, or because you have a working mate who appreciates and supports what you do, then this issue may recede into the background — but it can't ever go away, because our survival will be repeatedly threatened. Everyone is in this boat together — and this boat is called being human. Therefore, you will find yourself anxious — you can count on it — and your best response to this inevitable anxiety is dealing with it using the techniques offered in your Anxiety Mastery Menu.

HEADLINE

We are creatures with survival needs, and we are made anxious when our survival is threatened. Especially for a creative person, whose efforts rarely produce a sufficient income, anxiety related to sheer survival will be more than likely a regular — or constant — companion.

☑ TO DO

Really learn at least one anxiety-management tool that, via experimentation and practice, you know works to reduce your experience of anxiety. You will definitely need it.

VOW

I accept that living produces anxiety, and I will learn to beautifully manage that anxiety.

PHOEBE TEACHING TALE

THE NIGHT SEVEN MUSES VISITED

Early one evening Phoebe began reading a book about living the artist's life. It had the funniest, nicest illustrations, but the book made Phoebe feel so sad that she sat in a corner of her room and cried. The book was about the author's trials with depression and why so many artists suffered from the blues. The author suggested that an artist could handle her depression if she did the right things, but the message that Phoebe came away with was that a life in the arts was very hard and could break even the loftiest spirit.

However, it wasn't precisely the hardness of a life in the arts that was causing Phoebe to cry. It was the sense that she was lucky, accidentally and unfairly lucky. She had an excellent room and everything that she needed: music, books, canvases, everything. She had parents who loved her and who, in their eccentricity, loved creativity. She could go off to college or to a garret in Paris, and this comfy room would be here for her if and when she needed to return. Furthermore, her parents were certain to slip her a little life-saving money each month — they had alluded to that possibility already. Phoebe recognized what a blessing that would be to always have a little money for a new book, pizza, and cat food.

Her blessings made her feel guilty. It also put a lot of pressure on her to do great things, considering all her advantages. But after a further sniffle or two the guilt and the pressure receded. She was left with the picture of a million creative souls, sitting in cubicles doing corporate work, coming home too tired to paint or write. Maybe they got a little painting or writing done over time, but then they had to find someone to take an interest in their work. She couldn't help but picture a poor actor who only wanted to be a shaman having to cobble a strange life together of commercials and industrials and catering, a poor musician who only wanted to sing having to cobble together her odd life of failed bands and customer service complaints and addictions to painkillers and sedatives. Where was the beauty? Where was the meaning? Where was the point?

Phoebe resumed crying.

She loved some of the suggestions in the book,

although they were heartbreaking. Never spend more than a quarter of your salary on rent, even if that meant living in a hovel with a nest of hornets in the wall. Always manage to carry health insurance, to pay for your antidepressants. Make sure to own a toaster oven, so that you could live on grilled-cheese sandwiches, sometimes fancied up with vegetables. Hand-paint pebbles and barter with movie ticket sellers for free admissions to movies. The author had a hundred suggestions for how to survive as a lost creative soul. Each one made Phoebe cry harder.

As she cried, muses began arriving. Myrtle Mouse arrived first. A bee and a frog, whom Phoebe had seen before but whose names she didn't know, arrived together, making her think that they were a team, like police partners or a vaudeville act. Harold Spider appeared, then Monica Butterfly, then Adam Snail, then Melanie Caterpillar.

They weren't rushing, and they didn't seem distressed. Through her tears Phoebe watched them arrive. They hardly looked to be responding to an emergency. But that so many muses would come at the same time had to mean something. This thought caused Phoebe to dry her eyes and wonder aloud what was happening.

She addressed Harold Spider, whom she knew best.

"What are you all doing here?" Phoebe asked.

"Your tears," Harold Spider replied, "are the kind of tears that make muses respond. They are the kind of tears that cause creators to abandon their dreams and make sensible decisions. Now, we aren't against sensible decisions. We don't lobby. But we are available to listen and to suggest."

Phoebe wasn't quite sure that she understood. "Do you mean," she wondered, "that the book I was reading, which made me think about how sad so many creative people are, trying to survive and handle their depression and get even a little creative work done, might cause me to abandon my own creative life?"

"Yes."

The directness and succinctness of Harold Spider's answer caused Phoebe to sit up straighter.

"Well," she said after a moment. "I just wish that the facts of existence were *different*!"

"Yes, of course," Harold Spider replied. "However, you are not free to change the facts of existence, only to act for the good. If there are a million actors and three roles, you can't change those facts. You could, however, brilliantly conceive of a way for actors to engage in new, soulful work. You could invent new roles for creators, make suggestions, and be of help. But as to those three roles, you can't cram a million actors into them. To dwell on that is to invite sadness."

Myrtle Mouse squeaked up. "In the book you were reading, the author turns a traditional idea on its head. Instead of painting first and then finding picture frames that she can't afford, she finds the frames first, as cheap and as pretty as can be, then does art to fit the frames. She uses the metaphor of 'reframing' in its literal sense!

You too could turn ideas on their heads, help creators try upside-down and inside-out things, and help a few in that way. As Harold said, that won't lead to bliss and bestsellers for everyone. But you would be living righteously."

A discussion broke out about ethics, personal responsibility, and time management. Phoebe could barely listen. Many interesting things were being said, and she wondered if she were filing some of them away or whether they were going in one ear and out the other. But even that thought vanished instantly. Her mind was on its own wavelength, working out the basic equation.

The basic equation appeared to be the following. The universe did not welcome the birth of each new creator and say to him or her, "You will be provided for." Nor did it welcome anyone that way. You were just stuck with the facts of existence, with one starring role for every ten thousand actors, with a normally distributed intelligence that caused mass culture, with soap sponsors and corn flake sponsors needed for every artistic enterprise, with piles of unrealized work that a creator could only lament over, with…the word suddenly came to her…with, as the Buddhists put it, *suffering*. You were left with suffering.

"I believe I am now a Buddhist," Phoebe said aloud. The muses waited. "Or, at any rate, an appreciator of the reality of suffering."

She felt irresolute and muddy but no longer in the mood to cry. She put on a CD and let an artist transport her. With music in the air, she suffered through a long hour of French verb conjugation and a longer hour of Civil War memorization.

MORAL: If you intend to create, depression and anxiety will likely call on you. You will need some good answers.

Your Anxiety Mastery Menu

HIGHLIGHTING: ANXIETY ANALYSIS

It would be quite wise of you to become an anxiety expert. An anxiety expert is aware when he is anxious, understands the underlying causes of his anxiety, and knows how to deal with both the underlying causes and the symptoms of his anxiety. The first step is being aware that anxiety is present rather than denying its existence or mislabeling it as something else. Once you break through your everyday defensiveness and bravely recognize the presence of anxiety in your life, you're ready to deal with it.

You might start an anxiety-awareness journal, carry it with you, and turn an inquisitive eye onto your reactions to the situations that arise daily, whether it's deciding whether to jaywalk or deciding whether to work on your novel. Begin to recognize which situations provoke the most anxiety and how anxiety manifests itself — for instance, does it arrive more as mental confusion, physical symptoms, or cognitive distortions? Keep your journal for a month, and start to become a real anxiety expert.

One way to define anxiety is to say it is a reaction to a threat. Some threats are more real and pressing than others, and one feature of your anxiety-analysis regimen is to begin to distinguish between important threats, mild threats, and unimportant or nonexistent threats. The most important audition of your life is serious business, and feeling anxious beforehand makes sense. But sending out an email to announce your next concert doesn't constitute much of a threat. Nor does choosing your outfit for the concert. Yet people regularly get as anxious about the latter two as they do about the first. When you become an anxiety expert, you learn not to turn the ordinary into the threatening.

What stands in the way of your performing this anxiety analysis? Anxiety! Most people are made anxious thinking about anxiety. This dynamic prevents them from analyzing their situation and coming to smart conclusions about what triggers their anxiety and what anxiety-management tools they might want to use to reduce their anxiety. Try to bring some calmness to your anxiety analysis. Once you begin to think calmly about the role of anxiety in your life, you can arrive at some real solutions.

☑ TO DO

What makes you anxious? When you get anxious, what are your symptoms? What do you do to manage your anxiety? Are your methods safe, sensible, and effective? What might it be wiser to do? Figure all this out for yourself.

CHAPTER 7

THE ANXIETY OF DAY JOBS

A day job is a job whose primary meaning — or only meaning — is that it allows you to survive while you work on your art and your art career. Some day jobs are satisfying in their own right, some are completely unsatisfying, some are more like second careers with their own perks and their own success ladder, and some are simple dead-end positions that go nowhere and aren't meant to go anywhere. What they all have in common, to lesser but often to greater degrees, is that they provoke their own special anxieties.

First of all, they are jobs, with all the pressures that jobs entail. Even if your job means nothing to you, it is still worrisome when you don't perform it well and know that you will be criticized and maybe even yelled at. It is anxiety provoking and crazy making if your boss is a mini-monster who rules your life eight hours each day. It is a pressure cooker if you have to meet deadlines, meet quotas, smile at customers who are rebuking you, and so on. By their nature, jobs — even ones, sometimes especially ones, you don't care about — provoke anxiety.

Second, there is the worry — the anxiety — that you will have to work day jobs for a much longer time than you ever imagined, maybe forever. You are banking on your creative efforts paying off, and the more it looks like you won't be able to live on those creative efforts, the more the specter of day jobs remaining a central time-wasting, spirit-killing, mind-numbing part of your life grows. It is one thing to work a day job at age twenty-four while you write your first screenplay. It is quite another to work a day job at age forty-four as you struggle to find the wherewithal to write your tenth screenplay after the first nine haven't sold. Day job anxiety and creative career anxiety are inextricably connected. Your first day job may feel like a lark. Will your twentieth?

Third, there is the anxiety of time passing and of missed opportunities. How can you compete with other actors if they are auditioning and you are stuck at your job? How can you get in enough hours of painting to collect enough paintings for a show if most of your week is eaten up by your job and much of the rest of it is eaten up by you recovering from your job? How can you properly network if you are trapped at work? How can you put in enough hours to master your medium? — such thoughts pester you on the way to work, at work, and when, exhausted, you get home from work.

How do you deal with the anxiety of day jobs? One answer is that you cross your fingers that your circumstances will change, say, by betting on the lottery, or you contrive to change your circumstances, say, by setting your eyes on someone with money and landing him or her. Another answer is that you carve out a second career rather than settling for a string of day jobs — you find something interesting and lucrative to do that you invest meaning in, just as you invest meaning in your creative efforts. (But try to make sure that it *is* interesting and lucrative, or you won't have gained much ground.) And then there is the bottom-line answer: if you must work a day job, then you must effectively manage the anxiety that arises there by using the anxiety management tools you are learning.

HEADLINE

Day jobs come with their own set of anxieties, from mean bosses to the experience of time being wasted. Get ready.

☑ TO DO

Think through the following interrelated three-part conundrum: 1) Should I work a day job and do any art I like, even art I know is unlikely to sell, hoping against hope that what I create will in fact be wanted? 2) Should I work a day job but do art that I think is likely to sell, so as to increase my chances of one day being able to give up my day job? 3) Should I choose a second career rather than a string of day jobs? What are the pluses and minuses of each choice?

VOW

I will do my best to make sense of the role that day jobs play in my life — and if they must have a place, then I will effectively manage the anxiety that they invariably provoke.

PHOEBE TEACHING TALE

THE COMPOSER WHO STOLE TIME FROM HER DAY JOB

One Sunday afternoon Phoebe went shopping for a birthday present for her mother. She took the bus to the mall. Phoebe wandered aimlessly up and down the aisles of clothing stores, jewelry stores, a half-price bookstore, and a poster shop. Finally she arrived at the International Crafts Shop.

The shop seemed empty. Not even a salesperson was in evidence. Phoebe strolled among the rows of carved shields and woven baskets. Suddenly a display of stone boxes from Africa caught her eye. Almost instantly she settled on two boxes, a small, beautiful one in a blue stone and a not-quite-so-beautiful but larger and hence more functional one in a light green stone.

She thought that a salesperson might know what the smaller box was intended for. So she went looking for one. At the back of the store she drew aside a beaded curtain. A young woman of about twenty-five, reading a book that Phoebe could see was Voltaire's *Candide*, smiled at her but stayed seated.

"This isn't really the best of all possible worlds," Phoebe said, making a fine *Candide* reference. "Not if you can't find anyone to help you."

"That's because this isn't the best of all possible worlds," the woman replied with a laugh. "Unless you are well-heeled and completely conventional."

"Are you on break?" Phoebe inquired.

"Oh, no. I steal an hour or two from every shift

to catch up on my reading. If I didn't steal this time I would go insane. You would have to lock me up, and it would cost society thirty thousand a year to warehouse me, so you can see that I am helping society by stealing time from my day job."

Phoebe thought about that. "That's an interesting perspective. Are you an artist?"

"Yes!" the woman cried. "I compose. Classical-sounding music with folk roots. The only way I can go home and compose is if I am very absent here and don't use up my energy on invoices and dusting."

"I suppose you could be fired."

"Oh, I've been fired plenty of times. From the bakery. From an Internet company. From a bagel place, a multinational, and a temporary city job having to do with zoning ordinances. With that last one, I never even listened when they told me what I was supposed to be doing. It took them four months to figure out that I wasn't doing anything."

"I'm not sure —"

"You wonder if this is ethical?" the young woman interrupted. "I believe that it is. Here are the typical counterarguments. 'What if everybody did it?' Well, from working all these jobs, I would say that most people are already doing this, except when a boss is watching, so I am just being a tad more honest than your average worker. In fact, your average employee is doing considerably more damage. There were people working on those zoning ordinances who had no idea what they were doing but rezoned things anyway! Suddenly your bakery was zoned out of a commercial district, and you had to close up shop and move across town. Is that better than me not doing anything? At least I did no harm. 'No work, no harm.' That's one of my mottoes."

"I can see that in that particular case —"

"To continue. 'What if everyone did it?' Well, maybe things would change. Maybe Americans would get a life. Maybe they would demand six or seven weeks of vacation a year, like Europeans get. Maybe they would have the energy to go to a concert at night, rather than falling asleep because their day job is exhausting them. Maybe America would work half days and live. Who knows? So in answer to the question, 'What if everyone did it?' my response is, 'Let them!' Let's create a new America!"

"I don't know —" Phoebe began doubtfully.

"You apparently aren't moved by teleological arguments. You must be a deontologist! How rare to find one here. Most deontologists go to the Sorbonne and smoke nasty French cigarettes — though," she hastened to add, "smoking any cigarette is not very good for your health."

The Sorbonne reference so pleased Phoebe that she moved entirely to the young woman's side of the argument.

"What are those two things, teleologists and deontologists?"

"A teleologist says that the state can kill Joe so that

one day Bob won't kill Fred, so that Bob is 'deterred' from killing Fred. That's the 'end justifies the means' argument and the rationale for capital punishment. A deontologist says that there are always first principles involved in ethics, principles which you ought not to violate, even if you don't like the end result — say, Bob killing Fred — and so the state should not kill Joe, even if it would dearly like to take its revenge on Joe. Mills was a teleologist: the greatest good for the greatest number. Kant was a deontologist: the categorical imperative."

"Which are you?"

"Neither. Teleology and deontology are both flawed and arbitrary. I take a third position, known as 'my ethics.' I do what I think is right."

Phoebe had a thought. "What are you composing currently?"

"Right now I'm working on a trio for bassoon, oboe, and violin."

"And you play?"

"The violin."

"What if the bassoonist stopped playing right in the middle of a performance? Wouldn't that make you furious?"

"Not at all. I would say to the audience, 'The bassoonist has exercised his free will, is currently writing a short story in his head, and won't be playing with us. So this is now a piece for oboe and violin. Enjoy!' Would I work with that bassoonist again? Probably not. Would

I rant and rave about the bassoonist's morals? No." She glanced at her watch and jumped to her feet. "One afternoon hour stolen! It's time for work now. So — what can I do for you?"

"You are a very edgy salesperson," Phoebe laughed.

"I'm a free thinker, that's all."

"You didn't —" Phoebe had a sudden hunch. "Did you by any chance attend Lincoln Middle School and participate in the Free Thinkers' Club?"

"I founded it!" the composer cried. "I tried to start it in sixth grade and got rebuked. Fought for it for three years. I think there was even a time I had to have a meeting with a priest, a rabbi, and a minister before the school would okay it. Doesn't *that* sound like a bad joke!" She extended her hand. "Amanda Lattimore at your service."

"Phoebe Barlow," Phoebe said, shaking hands. "I just wonder. Why aren't you —" She hesitated.

"Better situated than this? I'm an artist with a degree from a fine college. Nevertheless, I work day jobs. I haven't failed because you find me working here at the International Crafts Shop. This is my fate, my destiny. I work here, I steal time, I compose. Don't cry for me, Phoebe Barlow. I am quite fine."

Phoebe made no reply. After a moment she said, "I'll take the blue one."

"Excellent choice! And since you've caught me between breaks, I will even wrap it for you. There are seven choices of wrapping paper. Come right this way!"

Feeling a bit unsettled and even a little sad, Phoebe followed the founder of Lincoln Middle School's Free Thinkers' Club back to the checkout counter.

MORAL: Just like everyone else, you must pay the bills. What a tragedy!

Your Anxiety Mastery Menu

HIGHLIGHTING: LIFESTYLE SUPPORT

Calmness may not seem like a great virtue to you. Maybe you prefer a life of excitement, adventure, and risk taking. Maybe you harbor the suspicion that calmness is very much like death. Or maybe you crave calmness and would love to live more calmly but can't see how to pull that off, given your chaotic circumstances. Or maybe you doubt that you have the inner mastery or the correct wiring to live calmly. Calmness may not seem like your cup of tea, or you do not believe it is available to someone wired like you or caught in your particular circumstances.

For the sake of your art, you will want to rethink your position. Calmness may not be your cup of tea, but just look at how recklessness and drama prevent you from doing your best work. Your life may not be in tight control, and circumstances may conspire to rob you of equanimity, but it is still on your shoulders to create greater calm for the sake of your art. Maybe you are wired in such a way that anxiety seems to course through your system no matter what — and still you must make the effort to breed calm in yourself. By creating less turbulence you allow your art to flourish.

How do you fashion this lifestyle? By making choices that support calmness. You stay put rather than run around. You quietly create rather than loudly resist. You refuse to manufacture unnecessary dramas and distractions. You visit with friends rather than make enemies. You love rather than plot revenge. You pack away your diva clothes in mothballs. You meet deadlines step-by-step, not at the last minute. You organize your space, your life, and your mind. You know what supports calmness and what maintains chaos. Make the choices that support calmness and, logically enough, you will reduce your experience of anxiety.

☑ TO DO

Create a lifestyle that supports calmness. This is infinitely easier said than done. Nevertheless, you must start somewhere.

CHAPTER 8

THE ANXIETY OF CHOOSING

Choosing provokes anxiety. Even such small matters as choosing which cereal to bring home or which television show to watch can create a little tendril of anxiety. How much more anxiety is generated by trying to choose between spending two years on this novel or on that one! Even more significant, every mark you make as a painter or word you put on the page as a writer is a choice: when you create you are constantly choosing, which means that a certain amount of anxiety will most likely always attend you as you create.

Should you send your character to Paris or New York? Should you add just a little more red there in the corner? Should you include this lovely scene in your screenplay, even though by including it you will be making your screenplay slightly too long? Creative people face these choices continually.

Typically artists are unaware of how much this anxiety of choosing is affecting them and causing them to flee the encounter. Our first line of defense against anxiety is to get away, and when it comes to creating it is all too easy to get away by not showing up at the blank page or the blank canvas. The anxiety of choosing will do that to us.

Accept that you have a million choices to make as a creative person, one after another after another, and that all this choosing is bound to provoke real and significant anxiety. The answer is not to avoid choosing! Rather, you must choose, and you must commit to your choice for exactly as long as it makes sense to commit to it. You must choose between killing off your heroine's lover or sparing him and giving her a happy ending: you can't do nothing, since that means you are not writing your novel! Since the answer is not to avoid choosing, it must be the following one: to master the anxiety that wants to well up as, day after day and year after year, you bravely choose and bravely deal with the consequences of your choices.

HEADLINE

The activity of choosing provokes real anxiety, and a creative person is by necessity and by definition someone who must make one choice after another. If you are not aware of this dynamic and if you are not careful, you will avoid your work or leave it too soon so as to avoid the anxiety brought on by choosing.

☑ TO DO

Explain to yourself that you are obliged to choose and that while you would love to make the right choice each time, what matters more is that you commit to choosing. The only other choice is to not create!

VOW

I will choose. It may make me anxious: still, I will make my choices.

PHOEBE TEACHING TALE

The Painter with the Painfully Blank Canvas

One Sunday Phoebe took a good book and a bottle of water to a pretty park three blocks from her house. The park had a walking path with benches along its perimeter and a dark forest at its center. Phoebe rarely went into the woods, but it was a beautiful, sunny day and the forest looked inviting. So she went off in search of a tree under which to sit and read her book.

After a bit she came to a clearing in whose center was a painter at an easel. He was an angular, bearded man of about forty wearing clean jeans and a colorful vest. In his left hand was a full palette, and in front of him was a blank canvas. He glanced at Phoebe, shook his head, and exclaimed, "What are you supposed to do with all this?" He waved at the scene in front of him, a dense tangle of trees, ferns, and vines.

"Why do you have to do anything with it?" Phoebe replied, drawing closer.

"Well, you have to do things with things!" the painter cried, waving his brush in the air. "That's creating. If you didn't do things with sounds, well, you wouldn't have music, would you? If you didn't do things with strings — in your mind, of course, strings being very tiny and perhaps nonexistent — you wouldn't have string theory. Would you? If you didn't do things with images, you wouldn't have paintings, movies, television, or advertising. So, you have to *do* things with things. Now, here is all this nature, and I am bound to do something with it — honor bound, you might say. I just don't know what."

"Couldn't you —" Phoebe hesitated.

"What?"

"Well, I was going to say, can't you just paint what you see?"

"I'm glad you stopped yourself! Of course that's too naive an answer. Paint what you see! How premodern!"

"You don't have to be insulting," Phoebe replied.

"I'm sorry," the painter agreed. He put down his paintbrush and palette and sat down beside them. "There's nothing significant out there," he continued. "There's only a person's response to what's out there. At any rate, that's the prevailing view."

"Quite," Phoebe agreed acidly, her feelings hurt. "But apparently you're devoid of responses. Maybe you should be in a coffee house talking with people about painting, instead of being here painting. Or, rather, being here not painting."

Tears sprang to the painter's eyes. "You've hurt my feelings," he said in a small voice.

"Well, you hurt mine," Phoebe replied.

"I'm sorry." He pursed his lips. "I don't think it's that I shouldn't be here," he continued. "I love it here. I think it's that I've got so many ideas in my head from other painters that I can't think for myself. I'm filled up with attitudes."

"Like what?"

"For instance, maybe I should be looking at the danger here. Constance Mallinson said, 'My work is the antithesis of Romantic landscape painting, with its notions of a religious sublime.' Ira Joel Haber said, 'Nature frightens. No slow early morning walks in the country for me. Mountains collapse, rivers reclaim, skies open up, and caves swallow.' That makes me think I should consider nature as dangerous and communicate something about danger."

"I see," Phoebe said. "That's interesting."

"But what about this? Robert Henri said, 'Rather paint the flying spirit of the bird than its feathers.' That makes me think that I need to communicate something about motion. Not the motion of animals, but the motion of the vegetation itself, like the way Van Gogh's wheat fields sway with life."

"Yes," Phoebe agreed.

"Or I could tackle formal questions. Arthur Dove said, 'I have moved from planes to lines. This happened one day when I tried to draw a waterfall: the line was the only thing that had speed enough.' Ben Shahn said, 'How do you paint yellow wheat against a yellow sky? You paint it jet-black.' Planes or lines? Yellow wheat or black wheat? I could occupy myself with questions like those."

"I see."

"Maybe I'm not supposed to do anything. Eugene Delacroix said, 'What makes for sovereign ugliness is our mean arranging of the great and sublime thing called nature.' But what would that mean, not doing any arranging? Should I just copy? But Jean Metzinger said, 'If we find the width of the river, the height of its banks, intact upon the canvas, we shall have learned nothing about the genius of the painter.' So that's the opposite view. Maybe."

Phoebe's head began to hurt.

"Maybe I'm just supposed to paint color," the painter continued. Claude Monet said, 'When you go out to paint, try to forget what objects are before you. Merely think, here is a little square of blue, here is a streak of yellow, and paint it all exactly until it yields your own naive impression of the scene.' Picasso too talked about disgorging color. Then there are the Fauves, with their red trees and blue mountains..." His voice trailed off.

Phoebe sat down beside him. "You do seem burdened by all these ideas."

"And what about abstraction?" he resumed. "Mondrian said, 'I, too, find the flower beautiful in its outward appearance. But a deeper beauty lies concealed within.' Is that the ideal?"

"Stop!" Phoebe cried. "I don't think the problem is that you have too many ideas. I think the problem is that you have too few!"

The painter blinked. "Excuse me?"

"I'm sorry. But it's true!"

"A painter should know art history," the painter retorted, but without much conviction. "You can't just paint a landscape from a hundred years ago. What's the point in that? You have to...go forward. Do the next thing. Lead the way. Right?"

Phoebe shrugged. "You're thinking like an art historian, not an artist."

The painter frowned.

"I think that you're just worried that what you paint will get criticized. That people will say, 'Well, it isn't this and it isn't that.' To forestall that criticism you're trying to cover every base and take every idea into account. But you can't. It can't be done that way. If you paint small, someone will say, 'Trivial. Ought to be bigger.' If you paint big, someone will say, 'What an ego!' Just —"

The painter hung on Phoebe's words.

"Well, you know!" Phoebe laughed. "Just do it."

The painter stared at her. His face took on a look of pained disappointment.

"It's not that simple," he said slowly. "Sorry. I need ideas, reasons, something to go on in order to paint. I can't just move my arm and lay down pigment. That would be meaningless."

"You're missing something." Suddenly Phoebe snapped her fingers. "I think you should do my portrait!" she exclaimed. "I believe that's the answer!"

"Your portrait," he murmured. "All right! Only... where should I put you? I could have you kind of curled up, but that might echo *Christina's World*. I've got to be careful not to mimic Manet or the parodies of Manet, or set you up in the style of Norman Rockwell —"

"Golly!" Phoebe cried. "You're making my head ache!" She laughed merrily. "I'm going to sit here and read my book. The rest is up to you. In two hours I'm leaving and getting an ice cream cone. Until then, please be quiet!"

MORAL: You can debate, or you can create.

Your Anxiety Mastery Menu

HIGHLIGHTING: BEHAVIORAL CHANGES

What you actually do when you feel anxious makes a big difference. Behaviors such as playing games or watching television for hours quell anxiety but waste vast amounts of your time. Behaviors such as smoking cigarettes chemically quell anxiety but increase your health risks. If a ten-minute shower or a twenty-minute walk can do as good a job of reducing your anxiety as watching another hour of golf or smoking another several cigarettes, isn't it the behavior to choose?

There are many time-wasting, unhealthy, and dispiriting way to manage anxiety. The one that wastes the most time is avoidance. The way that people typically deal with situations that make them anxious is to avoid them. If driving over bridges frightens you, you contrive to avoid bridges when you travel. If writing your novel, finishing your symphony, or contacting gallery owners about your paintings makes you anxious, your first line of defense is to avoid your novel, your symphony, or those gallery owners. Creative people waste enormous amounts of time this way — sometimes a lifetime.

Then there are all the unhealthy and dispiriting ways to manage anxiety: participating in never-ending dramas, using too much alcohol and drugs, picking fights, pulling the covers up over your head and hiding, driving too fast, volunteering your time away, and on and on. Human beings engage in too many behaviors to name in pursuit of reducing their experience of anxiety. I am providing you with twenty-two categories of smarter things to do to manage your anxiety, to stand against the hundreds and thousands of sad tactics people customarily employ to quell their anxiety.

How you behave matters. It is some combination of discipline and devotion to show up at your studio day in and day out to wrestle with the large painting that refuses to work. That showing up is the positive behavior you want to manifest. But it is equally a matter of discipline and devotion to refuse to engage in behaviors that deflect you from showing up. There are behaviors you want to support, such as actually doing your creative work and actually practicing your anxiety-management strategies, and behaviors you want to extinguish, such as driving a hundred miles an hour down country roads or blithely giving away the coming year because someone asked you to.

Always consider how you behave to be one of your primary anxiety-management tools. Ultimately you will reduce your anxiety more by showing up, getting your creative work done, building a body of work, and learning from your efforts than by drinking, avoiding your work, moving every few months, living chaotically, and so on. Over time, the first set of behaviors reduces your anxiety; the second set does not.

☑ TO DO

Choose to behave in ways that, even if they provoke some anxiety, support rather than undermine your efforts. It is funny to think that acting in ways that provoke some anxiety can be an anxiety-management tool. But just consider which actually does a better long-term job of reducing your experience of anxiety: getting your novel written, or spending a decade avoiding writing it.

CHAPTER 9

THE ANXIETY
OF COMPROMISING

You have ideas about what to create. But then many forces will conspire, causing you to wonder if you should change your mind. The first is self-censorship: the concern that what you are about to say (in your memoir, painting, song) is too revealing of your inner world, too revealing of some truth about family members or friends, and so on. The second are all the demands made on you by the world: the advice you get from your literary agent, the demand you get from your editor, the suggestion you get from the only gallery owner who so far has been willing to hang your watercolors. In each of these cases, you will be forced to think through just how willing you are to go against your initial impulse and compromise: and this conflict will produce anxiety.

Every conflict produces anxiety, whether it's a conflict with a co-worker who makes you anxious each time you return to the office or a conflict about whether to focus on your fine art or your graphic art that makes you anxious each time you try to make time for one or the other. The inner conflicts that arise as you decide whether and how much to compromise can make you especially anxious because often they both have a moral component ("It would be wrong to market myself in that deceitful way") and an identity component ("I just can't see doing that — it doesn't fit with my picture of who I am"). Since these involve both your ethics and your self-image, conflicts around compromising can produce some of the severest and most stubborn brands of anxiety.

Neither end of the spectrum works particularly well: never to compromise (thereby closing doors and losing opportunities) or always to compromise (thereby feeling and being treated like a patsy). Therefore, you will need to deal with each new compromise on its own terms, since you will have no principle in place such as "I always agree" or "I never agree" to fall back on. You will have to weigh your options, peer into the future to see the consequences of your choice, and decide where in the sand you want to draw the line. This weighing, peering, and deciding is bound to produce anxiety, and you must deal with it by having your anxiety tools in place — your cognitive tools, your breathing tools, your relaxation tools — the whole tool kit.

HEADLINE

The creative life will provide you with countless situations in which you will have to decide whether, and to what extent, you are willing to compromise. These situations can't be avoided except by retreating and by hiding. They must be dealt with — and so must the anxiety that comes with them.

☑ TO DO

Create a basic plan for dealing with situations in which a compromise may be necessary. The plan might be as simple as remembering to give yourself some time to think through your options and to write down the pros and cons of one choice versus the other. You might also want to factor in your shadow as you contemplate your choices: if you are characteristically unwilling to compromise, give a little weight to the possibility that you may want to bend some, and if you are usually too willing to compromise, think about asserting yourself more.

VOW

When a situation arises in which I may need to compromise, I will address it forthrightly and do the best job I can of weighing my options — and managing the accompanying anxiety

ARI TEACHING TALE

THE LITERAL MAN

One day a Literal Man came to see Ari. Few Literal People ever visited, since they tended to have no use for creativity and no sense of themselves as creative. But every so often a Literal Man or Woman had a vision, dream, or epiphany and wondered, if only for a fleeting second, whether there might be something more to life than facts and bargains.

This particular Literal Man came early, spent time in the shop behind which Ari kept his office, and learned what he had already suspected, that the prices of the shop were not as good as the prices he could get on the

Internet. This made him smile. He always liked it when he knew the best place to buy something, whether or not he had any intention of buying that thing. He knew the best place to buy vacuum cleaners, the best place to have business cards printed, the best place to buy Irish linen and Icelandic sweaters. There was nothing in the shop that looked to be a bargain.

At the appointed time, right to the second, he made his way down the narrow corridor and entered Ari's consulting room.

"You charge a very reasonable rate," he said by way of greeting. Ari waved him to a seat as he continued talking. "I think you could charge much more, if you wanted. Psychiatrists where I live charge three times what you charge. Business consultants charge five times more. If they have books published and have been on television, ten times more."

"Well, but they have different goals," Ari replied. "They are trying to help people. My goal is to disappoint my clients. So I charge less."

The Literal Man stared at Ari for a moment. Then he grinned from ear to ear. "You're making fun of me!" he said. "I guess I seem much less interesting than your usual clients. I have no talents, no dreams, and no aspirations. All I really want is a comfortable retirement. Did I mention that my mutual funds are doing very well? They went up eighteen percent last year. I could have done a lot better if I had taken a more aggressive route, but I figured, I'm not a lucky person, so I decided to stay with a mixed portfolio that's on the conservative side."

"That seems wise."

The Literal Man stopped for a second, perhaps to breathe. "You haven't asked me why I came to see you," he resumed suddenly.

"I supposed that you'd tell me when you were ready."

"And if I hadn't? You would have let me go without getting to it?"

"I would have asked you once or twice, probably."

"Of course! Just a little nudge, because it's my responsibility."

"Exactly."

"But just the tiniest nudge? So tiny that I might hardly notice?"

"No. I would have wrestled you to the ground and beaten the truth out of you."

"You're making fun of me!" the Literal Man said, smiling. "I know I'm not interesting like your other clients. That goes without saying!"

Ari laughed. "You take such pride in not being interesting! I'm not sure I've ever seen anyone take such pride in anything! You are a prouder man than my most celebrated clients!"

This confused the Literal Man. He opened his mouth to speak and then closed it again. "You're still making fun of me," he said after a while. Only now he wasn't smiling. He put his head in his hands. It was an odd gesture and reminded Ari of something from *The Death of a Salesman*.

"I'm ready to ask," Ari said. "What brings you here?"

The Literal Man looked up. "I had a dream. In the dream, my older brother was persecuting me. He always did that, so there was nothing surprising there. What was surprising was that in the dream I was a potter. I was a Navajo potter on a reservation. I've been there myself, in New Mexico, near Santa Fe, where you go into their houses and they have a little store in the back of their house, where they sell their pottery to tourists. It's not the way to get the best price, but it's very interesting, to see them like that and to talk to them. So, I was the potter, I made those black pots. I had a wife — or maybe a daughter. She tended to customers while I inscribed the pots. I was doing the inscribing for the sake of the pot, but I was also on display, I was like someone in the window of a department store who's doing something real but who's also there for show. I woke up very frightened. Actually, nothing much happened in the dream. There was something about the animals I was carving into the pots, the serpents and that sort of lizard —"

"A gecko?"

"Right! And antelope... it was all very disturbing."

The Literal Man finished. Ari said nothing.

"Well, what do you think the dream meant?" the Literal Man asked.

"I apologize, but I don't interpret dreams."

"But you do! You wrote a whole book on dream interpretation. That's one of the reasons I came to see you!"

"You're mistaken. I wrote a book about the mind at night, about thinking and creating while you sleep. But in it I said that people had to interpret their own dreams."

The Literal Man looked crestfallen.

Ari smiled. "There!" he exclaimed. "I've managed to disappoint you. You came with very few expectations, but I managed not even to meet those!"

The Literal Man made a small sound. "Should I go now? Can I get a partial refund? I mean, it's only been a third of the time."

"No. I'm going to make some tea, and you're going to tell me about the great project you want to begin."

The Literal Man recoiled as if shot. "I have no such project in mind! What do you mean? I work for the government. I have a very responsible job. I don't innovate. Even just to try something new I'd have to put in a DD 2840, that's a form we have for making suggestions and changing procedures —"

"Hush," Ari said. "Let me make some tea. We'll have it with lemon. The lemon is off the tree right there, the one you can see through the open door. You see the lemon tree?"

"Yes."

"Good! Be quiet for a moment and think about how

your brother persecuted you. Then we'll talk about you becoming a great artist."

"I can't —"

"Hush!" Ari said affectionately. "Let me get the kettle up. Then we'll do some real dreaming!"

MORAL: You can avoid having to compromise by squashing all your dreams — but what kind of plan is that?

Your Anxiety Mastery Menu

HIGHLIGHTING: DEEP BREATHING

Anxiety, stress, and the rigors of everyday life cause us to breathe shallowly as we rush around. Just paying attention to our breathing helps to reduce anxiety and is a core element of practice in many disciplines, including Zen Buddhism. Here is how Philip Kapleau describes the importance of breath attention in *The Three Pillars of Zen*: "Zazen practice for the student begins with his counting the inhalations and exhalations of his breath while he is in the motionless zazen posture. This is the first step in the process of stilling the bodily functions, quieting discursive thought, and strengthening concentration. It is given as the first step because in counting the in and out breaths, in natural rhythm and without strain, the mind has a scaffolding to support it, as it were."[1]

Many breathing techniques are available to you. In *Managing Your Anxiety* Christopher McCullough describes an exercise he calls "circling your breaths": "As you start to inhale, you slowly bring your attention up the ventral centerline of your body from the groin to the navel, chest, throat, and face, until you reach the crown of your head. As you exhale, slowly move your attention down the back of the head, down the neck, and all the way down the spine."[2]

Even simpler is the breathing exercise described by Stephanie Judy in *Making Music for the Joy of It*: "Anxiety disrupts normal breathing patterns, producing either shallow breathing or air gulping in an attempt to conserve the body's supply of oxygen. The simplest immediate control measure is to *exhale*, blowing slowly and steadily through your lips until your lungs feel completely empty. As long as you make a slow, full exhale, the inhaling will look after itself."[3]

It may seem odd that paying attention to something as automatic and everyday as breathing could really help ease anxiety, but it does. Centuries of meditation practice and contemporary mind/body research arrive at the same conclusion: that breath attention is an anxiety-reduction tool of real value.

☑ TO DO

Try out Stephanie Judy's simple exhaling exercise. See if you would like to add it to your arsenal of anxiety-management techniques.

CHAPTER 10

THE ANXIETY OF POSSIBILITY

Even if you do an excellent job of choosing, and you know that you are committed to this particular novel or this particular suite of paintings, an anxious residue remains as you consciously or unconsciously remember all the other projects that you are not getting to and all your other loves that you are not engaging with as you focus your time and attention on this project. Because you have significant appetites, loves, dreams, and ambitions, part of you wants to do everything, and the stark realization that it is impossible to do everything can cause serious anxiety.

In the beginning you may try to do your version of everything by squeezing in an hour of collage, twenty minutes of poetry, half an hour of songwriting, and fifteen minutes on your novel into the same day. But typically over time you begin to see that this simply doesn't work. Nothing gets finished, and you feel fractured and all over the place. So you decide to commit to one thing — and instantly feel anxious about having put all those other possibilities aside. Part of the anxiety is about having put all your eggs in one basket; part is about your fear that you may not have committed to the right project; and part is the "hungry-mind" anxiety of missing out on all those other possibilities.

The best approach to this dilemma is a cognitive one: remind yourself that you can create for a lifetime, that there is no expiration date on your creativity and no mandatory retirement age, and that, rather than operating from a scarcity model in which you "only" get to do one thing at a time, you will operate from an abundance model instead and picture — and relish — the body of work you get to create by attending to one thing at a time and one thing after another. If this approach happens not to extinguish every drop of anxiety that arises because you feel limited or restricted, deal with the remaining anxiety by using the anxiety-management tools you are learning.

HEADLINE

The reality of process prevents us from doing a million things simultaneously. It is hard to attend to more than one major creative project at a time, or a few at most. This means that the other projects we crave tackling (and that may seem more interesting than our current project, which may be slogging along) must remain undone — a reality that we maturely accept, even as it makes us anxious.

☑ TO DO

Get a clear picture in your mind of what it takes to create a real body of work. Such a body of work is not created piecemeal by doing a touch here and a dribble there: it is only accomplished when you pay attention to one project at a time, project after project.

VOW

I will serially commit and deal with the anxiety that arises from not being able to do everything at once.

PHOEBE TEACHING TALE

The Concert in the State Capital

Phoebe was reading the entertainment section of the newspaper. She read the reviews of several new movies, an account of the opening of a photography exhibit consisting of portraits of America's last-remaining circus clowns, and an interview with a band that, as part of their act, ate small lizards and toads. She read a review of a classical music concert that the reviewer had hated — he called the work "as irritating as an itch you can't scratch" — and the review of a play in which, as part the finale, rain pelted the actors on stage and the audience in the front rows. This gave Phoebe a lot of food for thought.

She was reading the announcements of upcoming concerts when one gave her pause. It was a concert that featured a famous Japanese flute player and also included "the world premiere of Amanda Lattimore's trio for bassoon, oboe, and violin, titled *Edge of Night*." Where had she heard that name before? Suddenly she remembered. Amanda was the composer-clerk she had met the week before at that little boutique, the one who, instead of waiting on her, had hidden herself away in the rear blithely reading her book. Now she was having her trio performed!

Phoebe wanted to go. She called her sister, Anastasia, at college and left her a message, asking if she would come. The venue was a place called the Old Presbyterian Church, to which Phoebe immediately took a liking. Anastasia replied by email that she would love to come, since she was taking a class in Japanese folklore. Phoebe's parents also seemed happy to go; and so a week later the four of them found themselves rolling toward the state capital as night descended.

They had a pleasant dinner and afterward walked to the church, which turned out to be a beautiful stone building with polished pews, narrow stained-glass windows, and minimal decoration. Phoebe was anti-Gothic and already knew which of the churches of Paris she was going to like and which of she was going to hate. She read the concert notes and found herself intrigued by the flute player, who had been born and raised in New York. He'd been a stockbroker until the age of thirty, living a fast and, in his own words, immoral life. Then he left everything behind, went to Japan, by accident picked up the Shakuhachi flute, and in the matter of a mere six or seven years had become a world-class player.

"Wow," Phoebe said to herself. "That's impressive."

The first half of the concert belonged to Amanda Lattimore and the world premiere of her trio. Because of their conversation at the boutique, Phoebe kept expecting one of the players to stop and announce, "I do not feel like playing tonight. I am going to work on my poetry instead." This expectation caused Phoebe to feel anxious throughout the performance. The trio was fine, she supposed, and the applause at the end seemed hearty. It hadn't, however, moved her.

The music that the flute player made with his bamboo flute was another matter entirely. Phoebe had never heard such sounds before. She didn't know much about Zen, but she guessed that whatever Zen was, this was its essential sound. Phoebe sat transfixed. In her program notes she had read that these pieces were the most classical pieces in the Shakuhachi literature, the same pieces performed by the wandering Zen monks of the fifteenth and sixteenth centuries. At one point Phoebe shook her head. She had simply never heard anything so beautiful.

There was an informal reception after the concert, and Phoebe made straight for the flute player. "You play beautifully!" she said breathlessly.

He was very lean, very tall, very calm. Phoebe had the odd impression that he looked like a bamboo shoot, that he had grown to resemble his flute.

"In the concert notes it says that you didn't start until you were thirty. That's incredible!"

"I did start late. But once I started I devoted myself to learning the flute. I practiced eight hours every day. Sometimes I would play just one note all day long, to really learn that note. I might practice one small piece for a whole month, working on my breathing, my fingering, and especially on deepening my connection with the piece. If you have the time and inclination to learn like that, you can start at any age."

"I think it would bore me to death to play one note for a whole day or one piece for a whole month," said Phoebe, shaking her head.

"Maybe. But whatever you decide to create, you'll need to apply yourself. Maybe not in the same way you would learn a musical instrument, which takes an extra amount of practice and discipline. But very nearly. I've heard excellent writers say that they can only write for three or four hours, at the end of which time they are too mentally tired to go on. So maybe there are different limits for different artistic disciplines. For me, I can practice six hours a day and not get bored or tired. You'll want to learn what your limits are — and not do less than you can."

"That makes sense!"

"Most people do less than they can. I did so much less than I could for the whole of my twenties. I had fun, I drank, I was lost, I did nothing that inspired me or made me feel proud. Yet in a way I was pleased with myself, happy with my fast cars, my fast life. It was undeniably seductive and thrilling. I was empty, yes, but also very smug and satisfied. If the emptiness intruded, I simply had another experience. I drove fast, usually in a convertible, a maniac and a menace. I loved the wind, the speed! It was love, love of a feeling, but not a love worth pursuing."

"Why is playing the flute more worthy than driving fast?" Phoebe wondered. "Ethically speaking."

"Excellent question!" The flutist paused. Phoebe half expected an evasion: a story about some fourteenth-century monk, a riddle, or an aphorism. "You just know," the flutist resumed. "Inside, you know when something you love is an indulgence and when it's ethically proper. No, you don't always know — I take that back — because it isn't a hundred percent clear. It isn't clear that playing the flute is more ethical than collecting food for starving children. Ethics is muddier than a person would like to imagine. But still, that's the only answer: you look inside, you decide, you try to make sense of the universe from the inside out."

"My ethics," Phoebe murmured.

"Excuse me?"

"The woman who composed that trio? We had a similar discussion just last week. She explained why it was right for her to steal time from her day job to catch up on her reading. She argued that the whole history of ethics leaves you with only one conclusion: each person has to decide."

"The whole history of Zen leaves you at the same place," the flutist agreed, nodding. "I can't say that playing the flute is moral or noble, but I have the sure sense that I could have chosen a much more ignoble path. So I'm happy."

They were surrounded by a dozen people waiting to talk to the flutist. Phoebe shook his hand and said her good-byes. In the car, driving home, just before she fell asleep, she heard the Shakuhachi flute again. Those notes seemed to find their way into the deepest part of her being. Maybe it was an illusion, another trick of human anatomy, that music seemed so true. Certainly music could be used to manipulate us — ask any movie director. But those notes! They just had to be true, beautiful, and good. With that thought Phoebe fell sound asleep.

MORAL: Rigorous practice is the surest — maybe the only — road to mastery.

Your Anxiety Mastery Menu

Highlighting: Cognitive Work

A wide variety of cognitive techniques are available to you to help you reduce your experience of anxiety. The violinist and aikido expert Paul Hirata teaches a technique he calls Half-Half-Half. The idea is to suggest to yourself that you release just half your anxiety, using the word *half* as a kind of mantra. You exhale, relax, and quietly say, "Half." You inhale again, continuing to relax, and on the exhalation say, "Half," continuing the process as necessary. In this way you never have to get rid of all your anxiety — you only have to get rid of half of it!

Another cognitive technique is reframing. Rather than believing one thing about a situation, you change your mind and determine to believe something else. The objective facts haven't changed, but your view of them has. For example, rather than feeling trapped as you get ready to be interviewed about your recently published book, you tell yourself that you have the freedom to leave at any time and skip the interview. You reframe the moment as one of freedom rather than entrapment and grow calm as you picture yourself walking right out of the studio without a care or a backward glance. (But don't actually leave! — that wouldn't serve you.)

The main cognitive technique that you want to master is learning to replace negative self-talk with positive self-talk. Creative people regularly talk to themselves in ways that are anything but encouraging and that provoke anxiety. They exaggerate potential problems, minimize their talents and inner resources, magnify small threats, and engage in other mind tricks that increase anxiety. Sometimes the negative thought is easy to recognize ("I'm not talented!"), and sometimes it is much harder to spot because it comes disguised wearing the robes of half-truth ("I'm too busy to create" or "I'm too tired to create").

The way to alter this self-sabotaging pattern is to actively dispute the negative thought and substitute a new, affirmative one. For example, the negative thought "I'm about to be scrutinized!" might pop into your head. If you've mastered thought substitution, you know to dispute that thought the instant it arises and replace it with a thought like, "Hey, I enjoy being watched," "I'm worth watching," or "Of course the audience will watch me! What else would they be doing?"

☑ TO DO

Try out one cognitive technique. Bring up a negative thought and then stop the thought by actually shouting,

"Stop!" Pick an upcoming situation that you know usually provokes anxiety and try reframing it in a more positive, less threatening light. Practice Hirata's Half-Half-Half technique. There are a wide variety of cognitive techniques to try: try one or several, and begin to get a grip on your mind.

CHAPTER 11

THE ANXIETY OF WORKING

Many different anxieties arise as we tackle our work. The three main reasons that we experience so much anxiety as we do our creative work are 1) that our self-talk tends to let us down rather than support us, providing us with anxious-making ideas such as "I can't possibly pull this off" or "I have no idea what I'm doing"; 2) that we doubt the quality of our work as we measure it against the very high standards of the art we love and as we strive to make it excellent; and 3) that the very nature of the creative process causes our work to morph before our eyes and comes with no guarantees whatsoever. Our self-talk, our desire for excellence, and the process itself all make us anxious.

Consider process. All day long you are supposed to get things right: drive on the correct side of the road, show up for appointments, balance your checkbook, appropriately respond to your email, and so on. Your whole day and your whole mind are aimed at not making mistakes, not making messes, not getting yourself into trouble, avoiding unnecessary risks, and looking right to the world. Then, somehow, you must shift from that way of being and thinking to a radically different state, one in which mistakes and messes are not only possible and probable but downright guaranteed. Of course that makes you anxious! And yet that is exactly what you must do, enter that darkness where nothing is guaranteed and where you may spend two years writing a novel that never comes alive or painting one landscape after another that doesn't match your hopes or aspirations. Despite such unhappy outcomes, that is exactly where you must go! — to a place very different from the place where you go to balance your checkbook.

Embrace the idea that sitting there and doing the actual work of creating provokes anxiety. Accept it. Do not hope for the process to be different. Do not crave guarantees, do not expect everything you create to be excellent (or even good), demand a certain maturity from yourself, and understand that it may be only every second novel of yours that is any good, only every third painting, only every ninth song. Hope for the best, do the work, and do not attach to the idea that success will be guaranteed if only you work hard. That is not life's truth. If you do the work, you will have successes: but it may not be on the project right in front of you. Yes, that makes you anxious! — and to deal with that anxiety, use the anxiety-management tools that you have been experimenting with and practicing.

HEADLINE

Creating makes us anxious. There are countless reasons for this, so many reasons that if we laid them all out they would stretch from wherever you find yourself to the door of your studio. Open that door anyway.

☑ TO DO

Do your creative work, even if doing it makes you anxious. Do not avoid it; do not talk yourself out of it; do not desire the process to be different from what it is. Do the work directly in front of you, the work you want and ought to do.

VOW

I will do my creative work and forthrightly deal with any anxiety that arises.

ARI TEACHING TALE

THE WRITER WHO CRAVED DISCIPLINE

One day a young writer named David, pained that he had not completed a single one of the twenty stories he had begun in the past year and a half, came to see Ari.

"I am so undisciplined!" David blurted out as soon as he was seated. "Please, may I ask you — what is discipline?"

Ari stared at the young man without smiling. Then he replied, "For an artist, the word *discipline* has a special meaning." He fixed David with his gaze. "Let's say that the urge to write about something welled up in your soul. What are your two possible responses?"

David thought for a moment. "To say no to the urge or to say yes."

Ari nodded. "If you said no to the urge, maybe you would go out and exercise. Maybe every time you said no to your creativity, you would exercise, this time jogging, the next time lifting weights, and so forth. If you did that all the time you might get very fit. What might people say about you?"

David pondered the question. "Well, I think that people would say...that I was very disciplined!"

"Exactly. But would you be writing or completing your stories? Would you be a creator?"

"No."

"For a creator, discipline means creating regularly. It can have no other meaning. Being disciplined in some other way, like doing yoga every morning or doing superb work at your day job, is not only not an artist's discipline but it may even be a person's avoidance of his artist's nature. So, you ask, what is discipline? For an artist, it is artist's discipline and no other kind of discipline, not even the very important discipline of the alcoholic artist who maintains sobriety or the depressed artist who maintains hope."

"I understand!" David pulled on his short brown beard. "But how can I acquire artist's discipline?"

"Imagine that you've been placed on a spinning beach ball and that you can just maintain your balance. It takes every ounce of effort to keep upright, every ounce of mental and physical dexterity. Could you also write?"

"No. Not as you describe it."

"What would artist's discipline mean in that context?"

David thought for some time. He imagined that if

he got very skilled at riding the beach ball, maybe he would possess the wherewithal to also write. He could picture a great acrobat twirling on the beach ball and also drinking lemonade and writing *War and Peace*. That image was very seductive. The great acrobat's mastery was very impressive and also looked effortless. Why couldn't he learn to handle life, no matter how chaotic and demanding it might be, and also write? But in the pit of his stomach he understood what riding on that ball would feel like. It would never be possible to write, not so long as he had to maintain his balance.

"I would have to fall off the ball first," he murmured.

"Or hop off!" Ari laughed. "Yes. On and off, on and off, one minute in the whirlwind of spinning life and the next minute in the deep quiet of not riding the ball. The first step is hopping off the spinning ball. Then you will meet yourself, in stillness, in all your nakedness, without that balancing act to distract you or occupy your thoughts. What will be spinning then?"

"My stomach!" David blurted out.

"Exactly. Then and only then will you get to create. Then you will find yourself in the very best anxiety, in real quiet, married to your own thoughts. Then you will write and finish things."

David nodded. He knew what Ari meant. But he didn't know how to acquire that discipline.

"Go now," Ari said before David could ask his next question. "You have the idea. Now master it."

"But —"

"Go now."

David got up reluctantly. A few seconds later he found himself back in the tumult of the bazaar. Just as he emerged from the shop, a shaft of mid-afternoon desert sunshine completely blinded him.

MORAL: For an artist there is only one discipline, the discipline of creating even while anxious.

Your Anxiety Mastery Menu

HIGHLIGHTING: INCANTING

I've previously explained the benefits of breathing and cognitive techniques in reducing your experience of anxiety. You can marry these two techniques into a ten-second centering practice that becomes a great tool for calming yourself. The idea is to use a deep breath as a container for a specific thought. First you practice deep breathing until you can produce a breath that lasts about five seconds on the inhalation and five seconds on the exhalation. Then you insert a thought into the breath, thinking half the thought on the inhalation and half the thought on the exhalation.

This sounds very simple, and it is. This technique is simple to grasp, simple to use, simple to practice, and simple to master. I'm adopting a word from the world of magic to describe these breath-and-thought bundles: *incantations*. An incantation is a ritual recitation of a verbal charm meant to produce magical effects. The magical effects here are instant centering and instant calming. The ritual is breathing a certain way; the verbal charms are the specific thoughts that you drop into your deep breaths.

The first few times you practice producing a long, deep breath you may notice that you're rushing yourself or that anxiety or stray thoughts are preventing you from patiently inhaling and patiently exhaling. If you have ongoing trouble producing a long, deep breath, you might try counting slowly to five on the inhalation and to five on the exhalation. Two unrushed counts of five should produce the deep inhale and the deep exhale that make up one long, deep breath.

What phrases should you drop into these deep breaths in order to calm yourself? Any short group of words that work for you! But I've found that the following twelve produce excellent centering and calming effects, so you may want to try them first before creating your own incantations. I've separated the phrases with parentheses to show how most people divide them up to fit comfortably into a deep breath.

1. (I am completely) (stopping)
2. (I expect) (nothing)
3. (I am) (doing my work)
4. (I trust) (my resources)
5. (I feel) (supported)
6. (I embrace) (this moment)
7. (I am free) (of the past)
8. (I make) (my meaning)
9. (I am open) (to joy)
10. (I am equal) (to this challenge)
11. (I am taking) (action)
12. (I return) (with strength)

Whether you use the phrases that I'm providing or phrases of your own creation, I hope that you will make this technique an integral part of your anxiety-management program. Marrying a deep breath with a useful thought is simplicity itself, and if you can get into the habit of breathing deeply and thinking a thought such as "I am equal to this challenge," "I trust my resources," or your own favorite incantation, you may discover your anxiety lessening tremendously.

☑ TO DO

Practice your deep breathing. Try out the phrases I've suggested. Then create a few of your own and try them out. Once you've settled on a few that you like, actually begin using them in your daily life as part of your anxiety-management program.

CHAPTER 12

THE ANXIETY OF THINKING

Remember how anxious it made you feel when you couldn't grasp an idea that was going to appear on the test? Maybe it was one of those word problems in algebra. Maybe it was a higher-order concept in physics. Maybe it was memorizing an interminable poem for an oral exam in English or pages of dates for a history test. Being forced to use your brain — to calculate, to reckon, to analyze, to synthesize, to memorize, to remember, to think — provokes anxiety.

Not always, of course. We don't mind a little thinking on the order of a manageable crossword puzzle or a simple sum. We don't mind thinking if the answer comes easily. But when it comes to working out the plot of our novel, that's a different matter. When it comes to solving an intractable problem in our scientific field, one that's stumped all the best minds, that's a different matter. When it comes to making sense of a welter of data, that's a different matter. If the results count and the terrain is tricky, we experience the same anxiety we felt when we strained to make sense of that diagram explaining how to put our bicycle together — only a magnitude greater.

As an abstract idea, we love to think. We imagine that it would be lovely to be brilliant while in the pursuit of some intellectual goal. But the actual thinking — not so much. So we begin a project with real enthusiasm, deliciously anticipating creating something lovely or solving some amazing problem, and as soon as the thinking gets hard we stop, our enthusiasm killed off by anxiety. We put the nonfiction book aside, pledging to return to it "when we feel ready." We put the research aside, announcing that it isn't quite as interesting as we hoped it would be. We deny or do not quite know that it was the anxiety of thinking that thwarted us, but that's what it was. People will do almost anything — not complete their dissertation, not deliver their book under contract — to avoid that anxiety.

HEADLINE

Thinking provokes anxiety. Embrace that reality; prepare for it; and get used to it.

☑ TO DO

Practice thinking. Choose a creative project, a research project, a personal problem, or some other task that requires genuine thought, and see it through to the end, planning for and dealing with the anxiety of thinking that dogs your days.

VOW

I will not avoid thinking just to avoid the anxiety that thinking provokes.

PHOEBE TEACHING TALE

The Substitute Teacher Who Championed Thinking

Mr. Pearson was the oddest of substitute teachers. Gossip had it that he was a brilliant professor who had left one of the University of California campuses to pursue some unspecified research. Several times a year he appeared out of the blue to teach a history, English, math, or chemistry class, and once or twice he had even substituted for Mrs. Gunbacher in German.

Today he appeared in Phoebe's history class. Since Mr. Pearson was, by his own admission, not especially interested in the subject the class was studying — the economics of Holland during the guild period — he opened the hour by posing a question.

"What is sanity?" Mr. Pearson asked.

After the requisite snickering and rib jabbing, the class fell silent. Mr. Pearson, a mild smile playing on his lips, waited patiently. He looked to be about forty-five, and his black hair showed streaks of gray. He wore a checked flannel jacket over a blue denim shirt, tough work pants, and even tougher shoes. Phoebe thought that he looked like a professor at a university for lumberjacks.

"What is sanity?" Mr. Pearson repeated. "Any ideas?"

Phoebe had plenty of ideas, but she was tired of being one of the few students, sometimes the only one, to voice her ideas, so she remained quiet. Mr. Pearson had asked a good question, and if no one wanted to run with it, well, she would just sit on her hands and hum little French chansons to herself.

"Let me get a show of hands," he said after a while. "How many of you are afraid of ideas?"

No hands popped up. But a few students came alive.

"Ideas are stupid," Zachary exclaimed. "We had a man come to our house to clean our carpets, and he charged $300. Took him just three hours. If he did two houses a day, five days a week, that's a hundred thousand dollars a year. What you need in life is a good steam-driven rug cleaning machine, not an idea."

"So you agree that you're afraid of ideas?" Mr. Pearson inquired of Zachary.

"No! I'm just saying that ideas are stupid."

Penelope jumped in. "People who think really hard always go crazy," she explained. "All the famous people we read about were half-nuts. You know that guy who said that God had died —"

"Nietzsche."

"He spent the last ten years of his life on his mother's sofa, never getting up, just moaning."

"God got him!" someone chortled.

"So," Mr. Pearson said, addressing Penelope, "you would agree that you're afraid of ideas?"

"No! I'm just saying that maybe the brain likes summer vacation and music videos a lot more than it likes calculus or philosophy."

This got many high fives and a rousing round of applause from the class. Phoebe frowned.

"So no one here is afraid of ideas?" Mr. Pearson wondered. "If I trucked out an idea, nobody would run?"

"We might fall asleep!"

"Or text each other!"

"But we wouldn't run!"

Mr. Pearson smiled. "That's great! I'm glad you're not a bunch of intellectual cowards, like most people. That we have a whole class of intellectual brave hearts is remarkable!"

Several students laughed. An equal number grumbled. Phoebe raised her hand.

"Why do you think that is?" she asked. "That people are afraid of ideas?"

"Let's let your classmates respond," Mr. Pearson replied. "Since we have a whole class of warriors unafraid of ideas!"

Phoebe shook her head. She knew what Mr. Pearson was doing, and she knew what was coming. Of course no one would take up his dare. As if they even understood they were being challenged! She'd been in school long enough to know that you only heard two things in a classroom: facts and opinions. She'd never heard a student — or a teacher, for that matter — present a nice, long train of thought, where a juicy question like the one Mr. Pearson began with was held up to the light of day and examined.

"I think it's *your* responsibility to help us see what thinking looks like!" Phoebe blurted out. "Our teachers don't show us. We don't see it on TV, in the movies, or anywhere! So of course we don't have a *clue* that thinking might be interesting."

"But *you* know that thinking is interesting," Mr. Pearson said gently. "Without my telling you."

Phoebe made no reply. What could she say? That she was brighter than her classmates? That she had better parents, ones who loved ideas? She bit her lip and gazed downward.

"Let's say that you got to vote for teacher of the year," Mr. Pearson said, addressing the class. "How would you choose?"

"The one who gave no homework!" someone shouted.

"The one who actually taught something!"

"The cutest one!"

Mr. Pearson went to the white board. "We call the things you're naming 'criteria of evaluation,'" he said, writing down the phrase. "So the things you think are important in judging or evaluating teachers are, what, good looks, amount of homework assigned, teaching ability —"

"Not teaching ability," Phoebe corrected. "Teaching actuality. Because a teacher might have a lot of teaching ability and still not bother to teach. We've all had *those* teachers."

Mr. Pearson smiled.

"And it would depend on the subject!" someone shouted. "You would never vote for a teacher in a subject that you hated, even if you liked the teacher."

"What should we call that criterion?" Mr. Pearson wondered, his back to the class.

"Subject taught/personal interest," Zachary offered. Mr. Pearson wrote it down.

"More," Mr. Pearson said.

Within five minutes the class had generated two dozen criteria of evaluation. There were sarcastic criteria, whimsical criteria, silly criteria, brilliant criteria. There were things like "height," "clothes," and "personal hygiene"; things like "kindness," "friendliness," and "patience"; things like "does the best job with an impossible subject" and "doesn't embarrass students."

"Now," Mr. Pearson said, "I'd like you to rank these criteria, from most important to least important. Get out a piece of paper and create your own list. Okay?"

There followed a bustle of loose-leaf binders being opened, pieces of paper being extracted, pencils scratching on paper. Phoebe glanced around. Everyone was working! She'd never seen such a thing in her entire academic career. There was no moaning and groaning. It was more like...genuine excitement! Even the rude boys were writing, thinking, making their lists. Zachary had a dab of ink at his lip from a leaky pen. Phoebe was sure that he'd never before been moved to strike a thinking pose and put a pen to his lips, not once in his life.

"People can be invited to think," Phoebe thought to herself. "This is very interesting. Since so few people actually *do* think, that must mean that there are just too few excellent teachers of thinking. And there's no subject in school called 'thinking'! No teacher feels it his or her responsibility to teach it. We've built a whole educational system, all these zillions of subjects from macroeconomics to ethnomusicology, and there's no subject called thinking!"

After about ten minutes, Mr. Pearson called for volunteers to read their lists. Almost everyone wanted to be heard. Mr. Pearson called on eight students and copied their lists side by side on the white board. Each list was different but also similar. "Doesn't embarrass students" was surprisingly high on every list and was number one on two of them.

Mr. Pearson stepped back from the board and examined the lists. He was smiling.

"Any observations about these lists or what they signify?" Mr. Pearson said.

Zachary, who half an hour earlier believed that you only needed a good rug-cleaning machine to make it in life, raised his hand. "It looks like criteria of evaluation are necessarily subjective, but there also seems to be some rough general agreement about what's important."

Phoebe was certain that a sentence of that sort had never before been uttered in any class at Lincoln Middle School. The class was thinking! She raised her hand. When Mr. Pearson nodded, she said, "I think Mr. Pearson should be voted teacher of the year. Unless a substitute teacher is ineligible." This met with rousing applause that turned into a standing ovation. Mr. Pearson smiled and said, "Since we are making up the rules, consider me eligible."

So it came to pass that Mr. Pearson became Lincoln Middle School's first teacher of the year, if only for a few minutes toward the end of one history class.

MORAL: Thinking can be encouraged. Who will encourage it in you?

Your Anxiety Mastery Menu

HIGHLIGHTING: PHYSICAL RELAXATION TECHNIQUES

An infinite variety of physical relaxation techniques are available to you that will help you reduce your experience of anxiety. In her book *How to Audition for Movies and TV*, Renée Harmon presents the following short progressive relaxation exercise, which she says takes about thirty seconds:

"Relax your forehead. Relax the area around your eyes. Relax the corners of your mouth. Listen to the sounds surrounding you but do not concentrate on them. Feel your arms and legs become heavy. At the point of the most intense heaviness, imagine that all your tension flows out of your body. Your fingertips are the exit points. Feel sunshine warm your stomach. Lift your chin and smile."[1]

Dr. Charles Stroebel, in his book *QR: Quieting Reflex Training for Adults*, advocates that you use the following four-step quieting reflex as your primary relaxation technique: "1. Become aware of the stimulus you are responding to (say a "what if" thought). 2. Give yourself the suggestion, 'Alert mind, calm body.' 3. Smile with your eyes and mouth to reverse their tendency to go into a grim set. 4. Inhale slowly and easily to a count of two, three, or four, imagining your breath coming through the pores in your feet. As you exhale, let your jaw, tongue and shoulders go limp, feeling that wave of heaviness and warmth flowing to the toes."[2]

Once you've chosen or created a progressive relaxation technique, you can follow the guidelines provided by Edmund Bourne in *The Anxiety and Phobia Workbook* for using your chosen technique: "Tensing and relaxing various muscle groups throughout the body produces a deep state of relaxation.... The following guidelines will help you make the most use of progressive muscle relaxation. 1. Practice at least twenty minutes per day. 2. Find a quiet location to practice where you won't be distracted. 3. Practice at regular times. 4. Practice on an empty stomach. 5. Assume a comfortable position. 6. Loosen any tight garments and take off shoes, watch, glasses, contact lenses, jewelry, and so on. 7. Make a decision not to worry about anything. 8. Assume a passive, detached attitude."[3]

Few of us relax very often or very well, and the lack of attention that we pay to relaxing has a negative impact on our ability to manage our anxiety. It would be wonderful if you could learn to relax all the time; but if you can't manage that, at least learn one relaxation technique that you practice and employ. It should go without saying, and yet it needs saying anyway in our world built on speed and doing: relaxing reduces anxiety.

☑ TO DO

Choose or create a relaxation technique, and practice it every day.

CHAPTER 13

THE ANXIETY OF RUINING

The thought that we may ruin our creative work may plague us even before we contemplate a specific project. It may lurk in our mind as one of our typical — and horrible — negative thoughts: "I am bound to ruin whatever I touch." It sits there as self-accusation and self-curse and drains us of our motivation to create. Maybe this thought has arisen because we have ruined many things or because we do not like much of anything that we've produced; or maybe it is more like a prediction based on comments we've received from our parents and teachers and from our own gloomy self-image. Imagine how much anxiety will arise if you are constantly saying this to yourself as you try to get on with your dissertation, stage play, or symphony! It is quite anxiety-provoking and self-defeating to suppose that you will ruin everything you touch — and yet countless people harbor this thought and carry this burden.

Even optimistic, confident, and self-friendly folks typically worry that they will ruin what they start. This is not so unreasonable a worry, since only a certain percentage of our creative work will prove to be excellent. To call the percentage that doesn't rise to the level of excellence "ruined" is a mental mistake — but an understandable one. It is hard not to feel that we have done the ruining when our novel bogs down, our painting turns muddy, or song after song sounds unmemorable. Isn't it an act of honesty to point the finger of blame at ourselves at such times? Who else could be to blame? So we disparage ourselves — and create more anxiety by attacking our talents, our abilities, and our very identity.

Since this dynamic is virtually ubiquitous, you must learn to live with the fact that you are going to call yourself on the carpet in the middle of your creative work as you begin to fear that it is already ruined or about to be ruined. It would be better if you didn't say such things to yourself or feel such things, but if you can't quite overcome these all-too-natural gloomy predictions, then you will have to effectively handle the anxiety that you're producing by predicting failure. Probably the best procedures to handle this anxiety are to breathe deeply and to do some cognitive work by reminding yourself that announcing ruination can't possibly serve you or your work.

HEADLINE

As they face the difficulties of creating, many people all too quickly predict that they have already ruined or are about to ruin their creative project. It would be better if they didn't think this; but if they can't help themselves, then they will need to manage the anxiety that is bound to nip at the heels of such thinking.

☑ TO DO

When you run into difficulties while creating, decide to predict success rather than failure. Say, "This will work out" or "I'm trusting the process." Maybe it won't work out — but you gain nothing by predicting the worst.

VOW

When anxiety wells up because I suddenly fear that I've ruined my work or am about to ruin my work, I will calm myself and return to the creative process.

PHOEBE TEACHING TALE

The Jug with the Snarly Lip

One afternoon Phoebe went down to the neighborhood pottery studio. Though she'd never tried her hand at ceramics, she enjoyed watching the potters work. The way a bowl or a vase came into existence was quite something. She loved to watch the spinning clay and the streamers of clay spin off as the potter used her tool to thin and shape her object. She especially loved it when a potter went inside the clay, turning a solid mass into something open. Sometimes the objects seemed so lop-sided she could not believe they could ever come out right. But usually they did. Only rarely did a potter collapse her clay and start over.

There were six pottery wheels in a row off to the right as you entered. Usually at least three potters were

seated there, busily working. Sometimes they sat together and chatted as they threw their pots or plates;
sometimes they sat apart and worked silently. Phoebe
wondered how they knew which to do, whether to sit
together or keep apart, but the matter of how they com-
municated their wishes remained a complete mystery to
her. Often there were potters doing other things, like
glazing their pottery or preparing the kiln, which was a
huge affair at the back of the studio.

This was a pottery collective, and a dozen potters
shared expenses. The big studio had a small walled-and-
windowed inner room where the potters showed their
work and held regular sales, always right before Easter
and Christmas, and a few other times during the year.
The showroom had no door, so you could always go
in, look around, and buy something if you wanted to
(and if you could find someone who would take your
money). Only during advertised sales was there a lot
of bustle in the showroom. During those times a potter
would stand uncomfortably by the cash register, ready
to take your money.

This afternoon, as Phoebe wandered around, a woman took an interest in her. Her name was Esther, and
she turned out to be one of the collective's founding
potters. Phoebe guessed that she was about sixty. She
was dressed in a black turtleneck, a colorful vest that
twinkled, and green corduroy pants. She had finished
potting for the day. As she dried her hands after wash-
ing up, she and Phoebe struck up a conversation. When

Phoebe admitted that she knew nothing about potting, Esther showed her around, explaining the tools, the vats, the stages a piece of pottery went through. Until Esther mentioned them, Phoebe had never heard of "slips," "bisque," or even "hand-building."

"Would you like to try hand-building something?" Esther asked. "If you like what you build you can glaze it, fire it, and take it home."

"I'd love that!"

"First we have to knead some clay."

Esther showed her how to knead new clay. Then she left Phoebe to her own devices. Phoebe found the clay interesting. More than interesting: arresting. It was like the cool mud in a riverbed, and also like tofu, and also, strangely enough, like the dry chalk she used to draw pictures on the sidewalk in front of her house. The clay seemed not to be on some continuum between moist and dry but both moist and dry at once, which was a little eerie and miraculous.

She wondered what to make. She thought about a horse or a turtle, but both seemed childish. An abstraction crossed her mind — something like a skyscraper, or an obelisk, something tall and skinny and tapered — but that seemed at once too modern and too old-fashioned. Then Giacometti came to mind, combined somehow with her town's own world-renowned sculptor, Garimendi. She thought of hand-building a face with the features just hinted at, the clay virtually untouched, the face sporting an unfathomable but probably ironic smile, something like an existential Cheshire cat.

But that seemed too hard; or was it too easy? She wasn't sure. Her head began to swim with choices and possibilities. To the demand "Just make something!" which she heard in one corner of her brain, she could only reply, "It's not so easy!" She realized that choosing was a dark secret in the underbelly of creating. She liked that phrase so much that she repeated it out loud: "A dark secret in the underbelly of creating!"

Finally she settled on a water jug. It would be Egyptian, a jug for carrying water to ceremonies, or maybe wine, incised and inscribed, with glyphs that only she could decode. The project seemed at once easy and quite beyond her, especially as to building and affixing the handle. But, tired of talking herself out of each potential project, she pounded her fist on the plank worktable.

"An Egyptian water jug! So be it!"

She worked for forty-five minutes, digging into the clay, modeling it, scooping out the inside of her jug, curving its lip, struggling to get it plumb or level or whatever you call it. Finally she stepped back to give it a good look. It was a fat, lopsided, ugly juglike thing with thick walls and a measly handle.

She wanted to squash it. Instead, she worked on it some more. The jug improved. It wasn't good — far from it — but it was better than it had been.

"Time to inscribe it! I will have fun with the glyphs!"

But the inscribing was no easier, and no more fun,

really, than the building had been. It was next to impossible to inscribe a straight line, no matter how short, or to make anything look the way she wanted it to look. Her crane looked pathetic, her horse horrible, her warrior bizarre. "The only ceremony they would use this for," she said to herself, "would be killing all the bad potters!" She sourly continued with her decorative work.

Finally she called it a day. At that instant Esther came by.

"That's something!" Esther said. "Ready to bisque and glaze it?"

"I'm ready to destroy it," Phoebe replied. "What a waste of good clay!"

"Why don't you fire it? Everybody needs a first ugly pot to look back on." Esther explained the glazes. "You never know exactly how a glaze is going to turn out, but this should get you an ocher glaze, very Egyptian-like, and you can do the glyphs in black or blue, if you like —"

"Black!"

"By taking a fine brush and applying the glaze in the #11 jar, the one that says Ebony."

Gloomily Phoebe began the process of bisquing and glazing her water jug.

After school a few days later she went to retrieve her finished jug. It had been fired and was waiting for her. It was real, ocher-and-black, heavy — too heavy! and — it was the only word that fit the situation — a disaster. The lip was the worst tragedy. It snarled. It was angry, ugly, deformed. If you poured water out of this jug it would spill to the right, which was just fine if the ceremony you had in mind was a postmodern parody of a ceremony. Hiding the deformed jug as best she could, she fled the studio.

She intended to bury the jug in the pile of clothes at the bottom of her closet until she could figure out what to do with it. But hiding it proved out of the question. When she entered her room she spotted several muses chatting away on her bed. They instantly spied her jug.

"What's that?" Harold Spider said.

"My first pottery piece," Phoebe replied, shaking her head. "It's exceptionally ugly."

"Your first pottery piece! Congratulations."

"It's *so* ugly."

"It's not ugly at all," Melanie Caterpillar said. "Plus, if you keep at it, you're bound to make beautiful things."

"Meaning that it *is* ugly."

"Every artist is burdened by the ugly things she makes," Harold Spider said serenely. "And not just in her past. Every artist has ugly things in her present. She may be writing a brilliant novel but one of her characters is unrealized, a mere shadow of what's wanted. An ugly blemish right in the middle of her beautiful novel! Or she may paint and paint and paint and feel just splendid and step back and scream, 'Where did *that* come from!' Or —"

"Oh, hush up!' Phoebe cried. "I get it!"

"Why don't you serve us some lemonade from your jug?" Harold Spider continued. "We could have a little party."

"The lemonade would spill all over! Just look at that lip!"

"Have you ever seen Van Gogh's early drawings?" Melanie Caterpillar said. "They're bad."

"Graham Greene traveled all over England buying up and then destroying copies of his first two novels, so ugly did he find them," Harold Spider added.

"And early drafts of Beethoven's symphonies!" the frog exclaimed. "Wretched things."

"And my own first poems —" the bee began.

Phoebe made a face. "Fine! I'll get the lemonade!"

A party commenced. Phoebe figured out that if you held the glass about three inches to the right, you could safely pour lemonade. The jug's snarly lip began to amuse her. "I have made an angry jug!" she exclaimed. "Better my first jug be angry than Pollyanna-ish!" The muses loudly drank to that.

MORAL: You will ruin many things on your way up the mountain. So what?

Your Anxiety Mastery Menu

HIGHLIGHTING: MINDFULNESS TECHNIQUES

Mindfulness means becoming more aware of the contents and activities of your mind and learning to do an excellent job of monitoring, influencing, and controlling those contents and activities. The best-known mindfulness practice is meditation, a discipline that includes breath, body, and mind awareness. Different meditation practices have different goals. Some help you exercise thought control, while others are designed to allow your thoughts free rein. If you would like to begin a meditation practice, you will want to examine a few different methods and styles to see which one feels most appropriate.

A simple mindfulness technique is the use of a mantra. As Stephanie Judy explains, "A mantra is one kind of thought pattern you can use to block negative thoughts. Often taught in conjunction with a meditation technique, a mantra is a word or short phrase that is simply repeated quietly, over and over, aloud or in thought. *Peace* can be a mantra, as well as *one* or *love*."[1] Is there a word that holds great meaning for you and works like a charm to reduce your experience of anxiety? That word can become your mantra. (For me it is a word that may strike you as odd: it is the word *process*.)

Reid Wilson wrote in *Don't Panic*, "Meditation is a form of relaxation training.... You learn to quiet your mind.... You acquire the ability to self-observe.... You practice the skill of focusing your attention on one thing at a time and doing so in a relaxed, deliberate fashion."[2] By spending as little as thirty seconds meditating, you can interrupt your negative thoughts and create a bridge between one mind-set, in which stress predominates, to one in which calmness predominates. In the blink of an eye, you can alter your sense of the situation and dramatically reduce your experience of anxiety.

Meditation is by no means the only way to achieve mindfulness. Any cognitive technique that helps you notice what you are thinking and that aids you in influencing what you are thinking is a mindfulness technique. Techniques from cognitive therapy such as thought stopping, reframing, and identifying cognitive distortions (such as our penchant to magnify and exaggerate problems, overestimate the risk involved in situations, assume excessive responsibility for matters not in our control, and so on) are all mindfulness techniques. However you decide to go about doing it, the task is to learn how your mind actually operates — especially how it produces anxiety.

☑ TO DO

Investigate the benefits that mindfulness and meditation practices provide. You might do this by taking a meditation class, learning one meditative technique and practicing it, or creating your own version of mindfulness. What you are looking for are results: that you really and truly become better at monitoring, influencing, and controlling the contents and activities of your mind.

CHAPTER 14

THE ANXIETY OF FAILING

It is one thing to write a paragraph that you don't like, to revise it, and then to like it. Although pain can attach to that first "not liking," few people would consider this scenario a failure. But what if you can't ever get the paragraph to work? — or the chapter? — or the book? This fear, which confronts beginning and experienced creators alike, can produce high anxiety.

What fears are actually involved? That you will be proven to have insufficient talent, that you will learn that you can't trust your instincts and your choices, that you will be forced to live that other "real job" life, and that your heart will be broken as your dreams go up in smoke. No wonder you get anxious at the prospect of a project failing and, by extrapolation and implication, your entire creative life failing!

Just as the easiest way to avoid anxiety is to avoid any

situation that might make you anxious (and by so doing becoming a recluse), the easiest way to avoid failing is to do nothing (and not have a creative life) or to do a million things in a flighty, frenzied, fractured way that amounts to never really committing. These easy ways do not please us, and we see right through our own devices so well that these methods only disappoint and depress us. We know exactly what we are doing: avoiding the anxiety we would experience if we failed, as well as avoiding the sting of failure.

Change your mind entirely about what constitutes failure. If you write three novels in a row, and each one, even after multiple revisions, still has its weaknesses, do not call them failures. How brave and spirited of you to have written those three novels! They are much more successes than failures, and if you can keep as your mantra the word *process* and the idea that everything you do is part of the creative process and that all you can do is try your darnedest and not attach to outcomes, you will begin to extinguish the word *failure* from your inner landscape. The way to avoid failures is not to hide but to change your mind about what constitutes failure.

HEADLINE

We hate failing, and our first line of defense against failing is not trying. Do not go this route. Rather, do your creative work and refuse to label any of your honest efforts as failures.

☑ TO DO

Really spend some time with the cognitive idea of reframing. You want to have a serious discussion with yourself about how to reframe the concept of failure so that the possibility of failure is either eliminated or at the very least greatly reduced. This is not a linguistic game but you learning for yourself that, through lack of self-friendliness, you have misnamed certain events and called them failures when they were not.

VOW

I will do my work and not worry about failing. In fact, I think I may just banish the word *failure* from my vocabulary.

PHOEBE TEACHING TALE

PHOEBE AND THE PHODIC SCULPTOR

Phoebe had heard stories about Antonio Garimendi that made him sound like a cross between Paul Bunyan and Pablo Picasso. He was reputed to have the strength of an ox. People likened his talent to that of Henry Moore, Brancusi, even Giacometti. Stories abounded: that he would sculpt for seventy-two hours at a stretch and then sleep for twenty-four, that he threw lavish benefit parties for good causes and let guests wander among his sculptures, that he dated notorious women, that he drove the back roads like a maniac. Antonio Garimendi was the town's only living legend.

Phoebe had heard about Garimendi from her writer friends Abigail and Michael, who were friends of Antonio. She had also read about him in *Sculpture Today* and had even seen him, not in the flesh but pictured on his elaborate website. He lived out of town on a spread made up of a main building, which looked like a Tuscan villa, and a multitude of barns and sheds. His spread too was pictured on his website. Every few weeks Phoebe would visit the site and study Antonio's face. He had a face built for smiling, but he looked worn and troubled. Phoebe wondered about that. If he made beautiful things, received praise, and was paid handsomely, why couldn't he smile?

One afternoon Phoebe dropped by Abigail and Michael's home and found the household in an uproar. The family was rushing off to see Garimendi's latest sculpture, for which Abigail and Michael's young twin boys had modeled. It was a private unveiling, and Abigail invited Phoebe along.

When they got to Garimendi's place they turned down a dirt road that flanked the main house and ended at a big barn. Everyone piled out, Phoebe trailing a step behind. They entered the barn and found themselves in an enormous space filled with sculptures in every state of completion. There were marble sculptures, granite sculptures, iron sculptures, and the occasional wooden sculpture. Garimendi was standing in front of what Phoebe took to be the sculpture in question, a stone one that seemed hardly chiseled at all, as if the boys were still hidden somewhere in the rock.

There were several minutes of commotion as Abigail posed the boys in front of the sculpture and took pictures while Michael and Antonio poured champagne for the grown-ups and sparkling cider for the children. There were toasts and comments on the sculpture, and then Michael and Abigail took the twins on a tour of the barn. Phoebe followed Antonio, who made his way to a distant corner where an enormous stone stood.

"My next stone," Antonio said. He seemed like a wild, sweet man who was also a tad on the anxious side, if *anxious* was the right word. "Look at it," he said, pointing to the rock. "Already it's so beautiful. Soon I'll start meddling with it."

"What do you think of when you stand in front of a stone like this?" Phoebe wondered.

"It's not what I'm thinking. It's what I'm feeling. I feel physical terror. This stone has something moving, beautiful, powerful, and true already in it. In there is a perfect sculpture. With my clumsy hands I'm supposed to bring an image forth. Well, of course, there's no other way, otherwise the stone would just sit there, beautiful but not the sculpture that it could be. Every artist feels this. Here is a blank page, perfect in what it already contains — the glorious novel, the perfect poem — and here comes a clumsy writer to ruin it with some average words. Here is the blank canvas, so full of potential that it makes you want to cry, and then an artist comes along...well, I always feel like I'm ruining things, not sculpting."

"But the finished pieces are pretty tremendous."

Antonio waved away Phoebe's praise. "Sometimes! But never is it the grand thing that was in the stone to begin with. Just an approximation, good sometimes, even fine sometimes, but never 'it.' I can't express to you how frightened I feel in front of a stone of this magnitude. I want to flee. I feel physically ill, scared, like someone is trying to drag me onto an airplane, even though they know that I am deathly afraid of flying."

"Maybe you're a phobic artist."

Antonio's brow furrowed deeply. "Explain that."

Phoebe considered her answer. "Well, when a person is terrified of innocent things, like the occasional spider or the occasional public speech, that's called a phobia. If you're terrified of the stone or of ruining the stone, that might be a kind of phobia."

"So," Antonio replied after a moment, "what do you do with a phobia?"

"I believe the treatment is called systematic desensitization. Or something like that. You get over your fear bit by bit. One day you just look at a picture of an airplane in a magazine. The next day, maybe you visit an airport and sit in the terminal for a while. And so forth, until you're actually flying."

"How would that work for a phobic sculptor?"

Phoebe pursed her lips. "Well…I don't know. I don't quite see the parallel. Would you just pick up a chisel, then put it back down? Take a tentative step toward your stone, then retreat? Make some kind of mark on the stone, any kind of mark, and stop for the day? I don't quite see how it would work."

"Walk with me," Antonio said.

They walked out of the barn into the fields, passing a garden of tall sunflowers, then a neat fenced garden of vegetables containing giant zucchini and plump toma-toes. They proceeded down a narrow dirt path leading into a forest. In the woods they came to a fast stream, and then to a metal bench facing the stream. Here Antonio sat down. Phoebe sat down next to him.

"The analogy doesn't hold," Antonio said after a minute. "And yet it's so close to the truth that I want to keep thinking about it. For some people, I think it's entirely true. They are phobic artists. They think of themselves as fools and failures, because they can't tolerate approaching their materials, the blank computer screen, the blank canvas, their own thoughts, and so on. They say, 'I want to create,' then they recoil, as if they had seen a pit full of snakes. It is exactly a phobic reaction. But why shouldn't they see it, be aware of it, and therefore have a chance to fight it? We know when we are frightened to fly. But do all these phobic artists — and I include myself among them, though my case is different — know that fright is keeping them from getting their screenplay started or writing their songs? They don't. Since they don't know, how can they be convinced or helped? And what would help?" Antonio mopped his brow. "Sometimes I go three weeks without daring to touch a stone. Of course, I may need that time to get ready, to have the right idea form itself, and so on. I may in fact be spending those three weeks doing something that prevents me from making a big mistake. But I know that's only partly true. Sometimes the whole last week I'm actually ready to encounter the stone but this thing — this fright — stops me. I get very manic and do crazy things instead. But at least, at the end of those three weeks, I do begin. What about the millions who don't? The millions who never fly, so to speak?"

"They must be very sad," Phoebe murmured.

Antonio got up. Phoebe quickly rose as well.

"I will do something new," he continued as they walked back toward the barn. "I will tell myself…no, it isn't about words. It's a feeling, just as fear is a feeling. There is a switch I must throw inside myself, the fear-off switch. I wonder if that will make me reckless? What if I had no fear? Would I just mangle my stones? Do I need the fear-on switch? Maybe I do. But what if I could gain just a little better control of this switch so that I could throw it into the off position maybe a week earlier, precisely at the moment when I knew I was actually ready to sculpt? That would save me weeks of agony each year. I have to think about this!"

When Phoebe got home she booted up her computer and visited Antonio's website. It hadn't changed — there was no message for her, as she secretly hoped there would be — and yet something felt different. She studied Antonio's photograph. She had no doubt that it was the same one as before, yet she read in his features a new expression. Phoebe was sure that some weight had been lifted from his shoulders.

MORAL: Locate the fear-off switch inside you. Learn how and when to use it.

Your Anxiety Mastery Menu

Highlighting: Guided Imagery

Guided visualizations are mental pictures you create for yourself. You imagine yourself in a tranquil spot — on the beach, in a garden, beside a secluded lake — and spend time there, in your mind's eye, relaxing and letting your worries slip away. To take one example, the pianist Andrea Bodo created, as part of a five-step routine to help her calmly make her entrance onto the stage, a guided visualization in which she transported herself to a spot beside a pool filled with water lilies.

Guided imagery is a versatile technique limited only by your powers of imagination. Providing yourself with verbal cues, you can visualize yourself calmly writing and publishing your book, acting or singing with confidence, or standing without trepidation in front of a blank canvas. In each case the visualization proceeds similarly: you seat yourself comfortably, placing your feet squarely on the ground, and close your eyes; using progressive relaxation techniques and breathing techniques of the sort we've discussed, you quiet and relax yourself, drifting into a receptive state where images flow; and slowly and clearly you pronounce, either silently or out loud, the cues you've prepared to produce the desired images in your mind.

Sometimes there's a person you know or have known whose presence calms you. It might be a friend, a former teacher, your grandmother, or a favorite aunt. It might be that one person who always had great confidence in you and would say, "Of course you can do that!" If there has been or is such a person in your life, you might want to create a visualization that centers on him or her. Picture the person's calm, confident smile, have a little conversation with him or her in which you're assured that everything is going well, or in some other

way have this person accompany you as you create or perform. If there hasn't been such a person in our life, you might
want to create one!

One musician explained, "One of the ways that I coped
with giving my doctoral recital for choral conducting was
by using positive visualization. Every time I became anxious
over a particular piece of music I simply visualized the piece in
every detail being performed beautifully. By the end of this little exercise, I was calmed and ready to move on. I was amazed
at how well it worked for me during the rehearsal period and
then before the actual recital." Guided imagery has this power.
Try it out — you just might want to add it to your anxiety-
management repertoire.

☑ TO DO

Generate a list of possible visualizations. Think about them
for a while, and see if one of them feels more resonant,
calming, or useful than the others. If it does, take the time
to turn it into a full-fledged visualization by writing out a
complete scenario with all the necessary cues. Then practice it and use it regularly to reduce your experience of
anxiety.

CHAPTER 15

THE ANXIETY OF COMPLETING

The primary reason that many artists find completing their work anxiety-provoking is that two events loom on the horizon: the moment when they must judge their creative effort and the moment when someone else gets to do that judging. Until he calls it finished, an artist can believe that the painting in front of him can't be yet judged. Whatever is wrong with it can still be fixed. Whatever it still requires will somehow be found. Since it isn't complete, no final judgment is needed.

Until you call a work finished you can maintain the hope that it will get a lot better. You can cling to the belief that you will solve its problems and turn it around. Because some percentage of the time you actually will pull off those last-minute corrections and transformations, this kind of hope isn't mere fantasy or wishful thinking. It is rooted in the reality that sometimes a thing of beauty can be pulled out of the fire. It is rational and plausible to maintain this belief — but only, of course, if you tie that belief to the actual work of correcting and transforming.

Since you aren't so sure you can pull off any last-minute magic, you find yourself dodging the encounter, which turns this piece of rationality into mere rationalization. You start to procrastinate. You find "good reasons" for not finishing: you've run out of cobalt blue, the weather is awfully hot, your mind seems to have left for the Bahamas. You tell yourself that you have no choice but to wait for inspiration. Instead of finishing your work, you do yourself in.

What should you do instead? Accept that appraisals and judgments are coming. Accept that forays into the marketplace are coming. Accept that when you're done with this project you'll have to deal with the prospect of starting something new. Accept that you'll have to deal with some loss, no longer having this project to work on, and maybe even something stronger than loss, maybe a whiff of meaninglessness as you stand in the void between projects. Accept everything that comes with completing, because you must get on with your work and complete it.

HEADLINE

As we head toward completing our work, anxiety mounts. Rather than trying to avoid that anxiety by finding reasons not to complete your work, deal with that anxiety by using your anxiety-management tools. If you don't deal with it straight on, you'll end up with a trail of incompletes rather than a body of work.

☑ TO DO

Look over the menu of anxiety-management techniques in chapter 1 and ask yourself, "Which of these will I employ when I find myself avoiding completing my work?" Pick one or two techniques, and put them into practice as soon as you can — that is, as soon as your current project or next project approaches completion.

VOW

I will not avoid completing my work just because the process of completion comes with some powerful built-in anxiety triggers.

ARI TEACHING TALE

THE FROWNING WOMAN

A new client was arriving in a few minutes, a woman ten years into writing her memoir. She claimed in her introductory email to Ari that she now wished to complete it. Ari sat thinking about those ten long years of not completing.

At the sound of a soft knock Ari rose and opened the door. The woman had a name   Susan — but the moment he saw her he dubbed her the frowning woman. He invited her to a chair and offered her a cup of tea and a fig. She waved them away.

"I'm writing a memoir," she said, frowning.

"Yes," Ari replied.

"I've been writing it for ten years."

"Indeed."

"I want to get it finished now. But my life isn't over yet, so the memoir can't be completed."

Ari smiled.

"I was serious," the frowning woman said.

"No," Ari replied, "you couldn't have been serious. I'm sure you have your reasons for not finishing your memoir, but it can't be that you need to be dead first!"

The woman frowned more darkly. "I certainly didn't mean that. I meant that I want to complete it, but I'm following a dozen threads in the memoir and none of them is tied together quite yet. They're at loose ends. But I think that will resolve itself in the next year or two."

"Good," Ari said blandly.

The woman paused, waiting for Ari to say something. He sat silently.

"Can you help me?" she said.

"With what?"

"With getting my memoir completed!"

"I don't follow. You said that when these dozen threads are tied up neatly you will finish your memoir and that should be in about a year or two. It sounds like you have a straightforward, crystal-clear plan." He leaned forward, poured himself some more tea, and brought the cup to his lips.

"But in the meantime...presumably there are things I could or should be doing?" the frowning woman continued. "I could, I don't know, almost complete it? Have it ready so that when the loose ends resolve themselves I could finish it in one fell swoop?"

"Fine! Let's come up with some excellent writing plans and strategies, and then you can go away and make progress on your memoir. All right?"

The frowning woman stopped frowning and started crying. She cried for a long time. Finally she stopped. She wiped away her tears and looked at Ari.

"I don't know what's going on," she said. "I just don't know. I've written thousands and thousands of words," she said.

"Yes. But that's not the same as really tackling it. That's not at all the same thing."

"I really do want to complete it," she said softly. "I want to share my story, even though it's painful...."

"If you complete it and show it to people," Ari said after a moment, "then people will say things about it and about you. Do you really want that? Be truthful."

"I...here's what's funny. I wouldn't care what they said about me. I've said that all already. But it would hurt to hear that they found the writing amateurish."

"Books meant a lot to you in childhood," Ari said.

"Yes."

"I'm afraid that you've put books on such a high pedestal that you've put your memoir out of reach. You've done a very natural thing, only without knowing it. You've made books into magical things that descend from the heavens. That's not where they come from. They come from a writer who sweats. Do you like to sweat?"

"No, I don't."

Ari nodded. "Where might your memoir end? Pick an event that has already happened."

She replied without hesitation. "When I finally met the daughter I placed for adoption. That happened a few years ago."

Ari nodded. "You could complete your memoir right now, if you didn't need it to be a masterpiece and if you didn't mind sweating."

She stared off. "I could do a sequel to tie up all the loose ends," she said pensively.

"Indeed," Ari said.

"So the problem has been — my high hopes?"

"Not at all! High hopes are lovely! The problem is the way you've married two thoughts. The first thought is 'I want a masterpiece.' The second thought is 'I'm not equal to creating a masterpiece.' You've painted yourself into a corner."

"What should I do?"

"Until you come up with the answer, you'll remain in that corner." Ari stood up. "I believe our time is up." Then he smiled and sat back down. "Actually, we have plenty of time left. What did that feel like, my getting up and sending you away?"

"That we weren't finished!"

"Exactly!" Ari exclaimed. "You know exactly what finished feels like! You knew it when you were three, and you know it now. And you know exactly what un-finished feels like. Work on your memoir every day, and at the end of every day say to yourself, 'Not finished yet!' and one day surprise yourself by getting up and crying 'Finished!' Work until you're finished."

"What if…" Tears sprang to her eyes. "What if I don't really want to write this? What if it's too painful? What if it's a cliché? What if it's terrible? What if I'm just avoiding —"

"Ah, Susan," Ari interrupted, "I think you intend to finish *me*!" He laughed brightly. "I'm happy to dance this dance of putting the memoir on the table and taking it off the table and putting it back on the table and taking it off again. I am very good at that dance! Does that dance interest you?"

"No," she replied after a long moment. "It doesn't."

"Well, then?"

"I think I know what I'm obliged to say. I intend to finish my memoir."

"That's it! That's just about the most beautiful sentence in any language! We may be able to get down to brass tacks now."

"We only have a few minutes —"

"Ah, Susan, the brass tacks don't take much time. Not after a sentence like that."

In three minutes flat everything else that needed to be said got said. As she was leaving, Susan turned back to Ari. "That was a complete session!" she said with a big, bright smile.

MORAL: The anxiety of completing exists at the beginning, persists throughout a creative project, and remains there even after the finish line has been crossed.

Your Anxiety Mastery Menu

HIGHLIGHTING: DISIDENTIFICATION TECHNIQUES
AND DETACHMENT TRAINING

Disidentification is the core idea of the branch of psychother-apy known as psychosynthesis. Rather than attaching too much significance to a passing thought, feeling, worry, or doubt, you remind yourself that you are larger than and different from all the stray, temporal events that seem so important in the moment.

You do this disidentifying primarily by watching your language. For example, you stop saying "I'm anxious" (or worse, "I'm an anxious person") and begin to say, "I'm having a passing feeling of anxiety." When your novel goes out of print, instead of saying "I'm ruined" or "I'm finished," you say, "I'm having a passing feeling of pain and disappointment." By making these linguistic changes you fundamentally reduce your experience of anxiety.

The Italian psychiatrist Roberto Assagioli argued that people become overinvested in and identified with transitory events (like an upcoming performance or meeting with a gallery owner) and transitory states of mind (such as the thought "I'm not ready" or "I'm not well"). He advised that the cure for this mistaken identifying involves consciously disidentifying.[1]

Disidentification can prove a powerful technique whose main purpose is not the "negative" one of listing all the things that you aren't but the positive one of locating your core strength that will carry you through every situation and transitory mental state. Assagioli explained, "When you have practiced disidentification techniques for a while they can become a swift dynamic leading to a deeper consideration of your particular stage of self-identification coupled with an inner dialogue along the following lines: 'I recognize and affirm myself as a center of pure self-awareness. It is capable of observing, mastering, directing and using all the psychological processes and the physical body.' "

To help this idea take hold you can create and use affirmations or thought substitutes that translate the idea of disidentification into useful phrases of the following sort: "I am more than the part of me that is anxious"; "I am more than any mistake I might ever make"; "My body may be acting up, but I am all right"; "My emotions may be acting up, but I am all right"; "I write, but I am not my current novel"; "I perform, but I am not my next concert"; "Whatever happens, the essential me will be fine."

Some people instantly resonate with the idea of disidentification and consider it their very best anxiety-management strategy. One painter explained, "I've been working on a solo show and had the usual problems getting the good work to come out. I started having thoughts like, 'Maybe this body of work isn't cohesive' and 'Maybe people won't accept it.' I could see how I was beginning to overinvest in the event, and I told myself that I really had to detach and disidentify. The affirmation I created was 'I will keep this exhibition in perspective. I am more than this work, and more is yet to come.' This helped me remember that whatever disturbing event is coming up will soon be in the past and I will still be there, strong and competent."

Disidentification is a technique belonging to the more general category of detachment training. One of the best ways to reduce your experience of anxiety is by learning to bring a calm, detached perspective to life and by turning yourself into someone whose default approach to life is to create calm rather than drama and stress.

You do this by remembering that while you can exert influence you can't control outcomes and by affirming that you are different from and larger than any part of your life: any feeling, any thought, any ruined project, any rejection, anything. By taking a more philosophical, phlegmatic, and detached approach to life (without giving up any of your desires, dreams, or goals) you meet life considerably more calmly.

☑ TO DO

See if the idea of disidentifying from situations and transitory mental states is a congenial one and, if it is, create some disidentification affirmations for yourself, practice them, and begin to use them as part of your detachment training.

CHAPTER 16

THE ANXIETY OF ATTACHING AND CARING

Life is about caring and attaching. We want to care about our loved ones, our causes, and our creative projects. We want to attach to our current project, pursue it with genuine neuronal devotion, and attack it with a passion that amounts to a productive obsession. Yes, we also want to learn how to detach and disidentify, as it is imperative that we not overidentify with and get too attached to any given creative project, since this project may need to be abandoned and that project may need to be turned over to marketplace players. But first comes caring.

With caring comes anxiety. If the project in front of us matters, if we genuinely care about seeing it turn out well, it naturally follows that we will become anxious when we have the gut feeling that we are sending it off in a wrong direction, making it mediocre, or otherwise ruining or failing it. Even on days when we've worked well we'll feel some tendrils of anxiety, just because we care, just as we feel some tendrils of anxiety sending our children off to school on a sunny day. There may not be a whiff of danger in the air, but we know life and, because we care, we worry a little — or a lot.

The answer isn't not to care. The answer is to care and to expect anxiety. That's the exact answer that every parent understands. You bring a child into the world; you care about your child; you accept that losing your child in a crowded department store, even for five seconds, will make you crazy with worry. Likewise, you accept that if you spend five years building a screenplay or a scientific theory and now it looks about to crumble, that collapse is bound to make you crazy with its own sort of horror, pain, and worry. For five years you cared; of course you will feel something! Even if you are very well versed in detachment you won't just be able to snap your fingers and make the worry go away: you will need to let time help — and the anxiety-management tools you are practicing.

HEADLINE

We need to care when we create. But where there is genuine caring, there is also genuine anxiety. Expect that anxiety — and when it arrives, manage it using your anxiety-management tools.

☑ TO DO

Engage in the following mind experiment. Imagine that you have spent a long time caring about a creative project. Picture the project, your emotional investment, your hopes for it — everything. Now, imagine that a day comes when you realize that your next move has a chance of irrevocably ruining the project. Feel the anxiety well up in you — and try to answer the following question. What will you do?

VOW

I intend to care. I will never stop caring so as to avoid the attendant anxiety.

PHOEBE TEACHING TALE

THE BOY WHO CRIED COYOTE

Idly turning the radio dial early one evening, Phoebe happened on a program called *Irish Music Today*. The show had just begun, and the announcer intoned, "In the West of Ireland, where the street signs are written in Gaelic as well as English, the band Bitter Fruit got its start in a Galway pub. From their latest CD, *Suffering*, here's a song called 'Woe Is Ireland.'"

An amazing song began. The lead singer was a woman with a supernatural voice who sent notes to places undreamed of by NASA. Backing her were Irish bagpipes, tin whistles, concertinas, electric guitars, and an array of percussion instruments, some of them more African than Irish. The beat made Phoebe tap her feet. At the same time, her heart cried as waves of Irish woe cascaded from the radio.

Phoebe felt that the song was helping her make up her mind about something. Maybe she was deciding to travel to Galway. Maybe she was deciding to become an ethnomusicologist. Maybe she was deciding that Buddhists were right about suffering. She couldn't say what she was deciding, but she knew for certain that *something* had been decided.

The tin whistle took its last solo. The piper piped a

last refrain. The supernatural singer sailed off toward the other side of the universe. The song ended. Suddenly cheering erupted, causing Phoebe to leap out of her skin. She glanced around and discovered that her room had filled with muses. Twelve were on her bed, six were under her worktable, three more sat atop her dresser.

She was about to say, "The song's over" or "I have to study" or something else that might empty the room, when a faint cry penetrated from outside.

"Coyote!'

Phoebe went to the window and opened it. A boy came rushing down the street, his hands cupping his lips, crying: "Coyote!" He was heading in Phoebe's direction. As he got closer, his "Coyote!" grew louder and more alarming.

"What are you doing?" Phoebe called down as the boy passed underneath.

"Warning people!" the boy yelled back. He looked to be about thirteen or fourteen. His arms and legs were painfully thin, and his hair stood up like pine needles poked into his scalp.

"About coyotes?" Phoebe asked. "Are there coyotes around?"

"No! I'm warning them about lying! There's so much lying going on. We're drowning in lies!"

"What sort of lying do you mean?"

"Lying about everything! Santa Claus. Corporate bookkeeping. Politics. Pop music lies. Churches lie. Whole industries are nothing but lies. Advertising. Fashion. Lies Republicans tell. Lies Democrats tell. Lies labor tells. Lies management tells. Lies drug companies tell. Lies homeopaths tell. Lies —"

"Wait!" Phoebe cried. "I'll be right down."

She hopped into her shoes, sending muses scattering, and threw on her coat. She flew down the stairs and out the door.

The boy had taken off again. Phoebe rushed after him.

"This is like a performance piece," she said admiringly as she caught up with him. "Like those action painters in Germany who cut themselves with ski blades in public bloodlettings. To remind their fellow citizens that fascism was not dead. This is very interesting!"

The boy seemed not to be listening. He was crying "Coyote!" again.

"What do you hope to accomplish?" Phoebe inquired, a little irked by his lack of attention. "Since no one is going to understand what your coyote cry means."

The boy stopped short and turned to her.

"It came to me in a dream," he said. "That I was supposed to do this. I think people will be reminded of the story of the boy who cried wolf, which might cause them to think about the lies people tell, which might cause them to lie a little less."

"Subtle," Phoebe said. "I like it."

Tears welled up in the boy's eyes.

"What's the matter?" Phoebe asked.

"My sister died of leukemia last month. Supposedly

she can't go to heaven because she never believed in God. That's the lie our reverend told my parents, who are crazy with grief already. My mother is pulling her hair out. My father's beautiful brown hair turned gray overnight. That Cindy died is horrible enough, but the thought that she must spend eternity in hell is more than my parents can bear. I know why people tell their lies, but they've got to stop!" The boy broke down and began sobbing.

Phoebe put her arm around the boy's shoulder. "You don't believe that lie, do you?" she whispered. "Hell is one big fat lie, you know. A horrible, horrible lie. Of course it is."

"My parents believe it! My mother is furious with Cindy for never believing, for getting herself sent to hell. My father is running around trying to see if there's something he can do to get her into heaven, if maybe she's in Limbo and there's still a chance. He's begging them to let him know if there's some special prayer he can learn, some offering he can make. My heart is broken."

"Come with me," Phoebe said.

She marched the boy back to her house and ushered him inside. They passed her parents, who were sitting in the living room. They gave Phoebe a raised-eyebrow look, and she shook her head. She led the boy back to her room, sat him down on her bed, and fell into her beanbag chair.

"Tell me about Cindy," she said.

After a moment the boy replied, "She was very

beautiful inside. When you get sick young I think it makes you kinder, more generous. She was very good. Her eyes smiled. She had a lot of love in her. Toward the end people cried just looking at her. They couldn't help it. They saw what a shame it was, what a waste that she was going to die. When you started to cry she would just say, 'Don't worry. It's all right.'"

Tears were in Phoebe's eyes. She heard a sound that she couldn't identify.

"What's that noise?" the boy said.

Phoebe listened harder. Suddenly she understood. It was the muses crying. She couldn't see them, but she could tell that a great many muses were around, sobbing and lamenting.

"It's nothing," Phoebe said. "Just our old pipes."

The boy kept listening. "I've never heard a sound like that. Are you sure it's your pipes? It sounds more like... singing."

"It could be singing," Phoebe said. "Sometimes our walls pick up singing. Our bathtub too. It's an old claw-foot tub, and when you take a bath, there always seems to be singing around."

"I've never heard of that before," the boy said. "You're not lying to me?"

"Well, I made that up about the walls singing. But what I believe to be the truth is too strange and too unlikely, so I'll keep that to myself. Then I won't chance lying."

"Tell me," the boy insisted.

Phoebe shrugged. "Muses visit me. Several are in this room right now. What you're hearing are a number of muses crying over the death of your sister."

The boy thought about that. "I think I'll write a poem," he said. "A poem for Cindy. I want to tell her some things. I don't mean literally, because she's dead and finished and can't hear me. But maybe it's like your muses. Maybe it's something other than the truth or a lie. Maybe it's just an acknowledgment of mystery. I don't mind mystery. It's just the flat-out lies people tell, when they know better!"

"You should go home," Phoebe said quietly. "Your parents are probably worried about you."

"It's so hard to be there," the boy replied.

"You could go to your room and write your poem."

"I could do that," the boy said. "I think I'll do that."

The boy left. Phoebe listened at the window. The night was silent. After a while she went off to tell her parents that she loved them.

MORAL: Caring produces tragedies. Not caring is death itself.

Your Anxiety Mastery Menu

HIGHLIGHTING: AFFIRMATIONS AND PRAYERS

Affirmations are very useful tools that you use to change the way you think. Affirmations are step three in the three-step cognitive restructuring process that I described previously — monitor your thoughts, dispute the ones that don't serve you, and substitute more affirmative thoughts. They can be used to replace a negative thought, or they can stand alone, in the absence of any particular negative thought, to help you feel more capable, confident, and calm.

Affirmations are simply positive thoughts that you substitute for any negative or anxiety-producing language you may consciously or unconsciously be using. You affirm that you have no need to worry. You acknowledge your strengths rather than focusing on your weaknesses. You applaud rather than disparage yourself. You affirm that you are equal to handling the ups and downs of the creative process and the rigors of the creative life. You say yes to life instead of no. You use the power of positive suggestion to block and even extinguish negative thoughts and give yourself an emotional boost.

Any short declarative statement can serve as a useful affirmation. Any of the following may work for you: "I am equal to this"; "I know my job"; "No problem"; "I can do this"; "I am calm and capable"; "I want to do this"; "I'm ready." Affirmations of this sort serve a dual purpose. First, they positively reframe the moment, calming and encouraging you. Second, they serve to alter and improve your self-image by providing you with new, positive self-talk that will actually take hold over time. One day you'll say "I feel fine" or "I can do this" and discover that, rather than uttering a hope or a prayer, you are speaking the literal truth.

Prayers or phrases from philosophical or religious traditions can work like affirmations to calm and soothe you. In the Christian tradition, any of the following might be employed as an affirmation: "Do not be afraid; do not be discouraged" (Deuteronomy 31:8); "Say no to fearful hearts, be strong, do not fear" (Isaiah 41:10a); "The Lord is the stronghold of my life; of whom shall I be afraid?" (Psalm 27:1); "I am with you; do not be dismayed" (Isaiah 35:3–4). Any combination of words with the power to calm you, whether you call them prayers, affirmations, incantations, thought substitutes, or something else, are exceptionally valable tools in your anxiety-management tool kit.

☑ TO DO

Create several affirmations — or at least one — that you can use as substitutes for the thoughts that provoke anxiety.

CHAPTER 17

THE ANXIETY OF
EGO BRUISING

We like to think well of ourselves (even as we often surreptitiously bad-mouth ourselves), and we do not like to put ourselves in positions where our ego may get bruised. This is why public speaking is the world's number one phobia (a phobia simply being a very serious anxiety reaction): because nowhere do we feel more exposed to having our ego bruised. The two ego bruisers that creative people must contend with all the time, rejection and criticism, provoke a tremendous amount of anxiety and can't be avoided. The only way to avoid rejection and criticism is never to enter the arena — which will provoke its own anxiety!

We are very tricky creatures and use all sorts of defenses to avoid getting our egos bruised. We deny that we just made a big mistake. We rationalize away our contribution to our lost years of not creating. We blame others for our lack of success, refusing to admit that we never had the patience to revise our novels or the courage to boldly enter the art marketplace. We defend ourselves in these ways because we know just how painful it will prove and just how much anxiety it will generate to acknowledge that we failed ourselves and contributed to our lack of success. To avoid that pain and anxiety, we trade self-delusion for self-awareness.

Worry less about looking good to yourself and more about honoring your commitments to yourself and fulfilling your goals and realizing your dreams. Look in the mirror more, even if that bruises your ego and raises your anxiety. See where you need to grow, change, and do more. Reflect on the marketplace feedback you've gotten, feedback that may amount to only rude opinion in most cases but that may, here and there, provide you with volumes of information. Do not fear provoking your own anxiety as you engage in this difficult and quite likely painful process of self-evaluation — you are learning how to manage that anxiety and do not need to fear it. Better to learn that you must change and do things differently and feel queasy at hearing that news than to do nothing and not have the creative life you've always wanted.

HEADLINE

We do not like to get our egos bruised. That is human nature. The creative life, however, comes with a lot of ego bruising: prepare for it, accept it, and learn to deal with it.

☑ TO DO

See if you can lower your defenses enough to identify one area where you really ought to change and grow. If you can manage to do the courageous work of self-analysis, institute the changes you need to make and deal with any anxiety that this difficult process raises.

VOW

I will not defensively refuse to learn what I need to learn about myself, even if that knowledge hurts and provokes anxiety.

ARI TEACHING TALE

THE WRITER WHO WOULDN'T REVEAL HERSELF

"Probably you don't really know anything," Sophie began. She was a woman of about thirty who wore a nose ring and a backpack and had been writing a novel for six years without making much — or any — progress. "Probably you are just good at building a reputation, like all gurus."

Ari smiled. "So, what is your novel about?"

"I don't want to talk about my novel. I don't know you well enough for that. Plus, that isn't relevant. I want to know what you think you can teach me."

"I think I can teach you that anger is a beautiful thing, if you are honest with yourself."

Sophie made a face. "What is that supposed to mean? Am I paying good money for stupid riddles?"

"You are so angry that you would blow up the world if you could. But you would do it like a sleepwalker, without any awareness. Then you would be angry at the world for not existing."

"Just what kind of crap are you selling?"

Ari sat back. The tinkle of bells could be heard as someone entered the shop at the front of the building. He shut his eyes. Then he opened them and stared at the young woman.

"You agree that you are furious with me?" he asked.

"You didn't have any right to ask me about my work! That's not what I had in mind. I wanted you to help me set up a writing schedule, maybe teach me some techniques for arranging my writing day. That sort of thing!"

"You didn't want intimacy."

"No."

"Nor do I!" Ari exclaimed suddenly. "You want to blame me because you aren't writing? Nothing could be more ridiculous! You want to blame your mother and your father? Fine, go ahead! You want to blame your God? Excellent! Do all the blaming you like."

"I'm leaving," Sophie cried out. She fumbled her notebook into her backpack, stood up, and put her backpack on.

"I expected more from you," she whispered.

"I expected more from you," Ari replied stonily.

When she was gone Ari smiled broadly. He made himself a cup of coffee and sat by the open back door. The dwarf lemon tree directly opposite him was filled with such plump fruit that the tree seemed to sag.

After a while Maya, who ran the shop in the front, joined him.

"Your client left quickly," she said. "You couldn't help her?"

He shrugged. "She is used to hiring people, then presuming that they will play a game with her. First, they will encourage her. Then they will get frustrated with her. Then either they will fire her or she will fire them. She has been buying scapegoats. She frustrates them, she is aggressive with them, she hates them, and all the while she does no writing. If she is lucky, one day she will see that she has a broken heart."

"You couldn't help her see that?"

"No. She came in with the energy of a murderer. At such times the teacher must exclaim, 'No, I refuse to let you kill me!' "

"You couldn't disarm her? Soothe her? Somehow find the right words? After all, you are the master, and you failed her. Where can she turn next?"

"To herself. That is my hope. I hope I made her think, even if just for a split second."

"I don't know if I like this," Maya said. "It sounds dangerous. Maybe even a little cruel."

"You never know about a pail of ice water in the face," Ari replied. "Sometimes it only makes you wild-eyed with fury and even gloomier than before. But sometimes it shocks you awake."

Maya shook her head. "I can't say that this is my favorite method of yours. I don't see the heart in it, the helping hand, the goodness."

"Remember, the woman came to me. When I saw

that we couldn't work together, I told her that immediately and charged her nothing."

"I suppose. But it's nobody's finest hour."

Ari smiled. "You're quite wrong! It's your finest hour, my compassionate daughter."

MORAL: If you stay guarded you can avoid bruising your ego. But at what cost?

Your Anxiety Mastery Menu

HIGHLIGHTING: CEREMONIES AND RITUALS

Creating and using a ceremony or ritual is a simple but powerful way to reduce your anxiety. For many people lowering the lights, lighting candles, putting on soothing music, and in other ways ceremonially creating a calming environment helps significantly.

One particularly useful ceremony is one that you create to mark the movement from ordinary life to creating time. You might use an incantation like "I am completely stopping" in a ritual or ceremonial way to help you move from the rush of everyday life to the quiet of your creative work, repeating it a few times so that you actually do stop, grow quiet, and move calmly and effortlessly into the trance of working.

The simplest and no doubt oldest sort of calming ritual involves the use of a good-luck charm. Soprano Lily Pons, for instance, would cut off a piece of the stage curtain to hold onto before each performance. Luciano Pavarotti, plagued by performance anxiety, looked for a bent nail backstage and reputedly would not go on unless he found one. Naturally, bent nails were placed everywhere backstage so as to avoid cancellations!

As Douglas Hunt explained in *No More Fears*, "The simple faith that a good-luck charm will carry one through is a time-honored way to handle anxiety. Often faith in an object lowers anxiety and fear and things consequently go better. Superstitions may seem out of place in modern society but if not carried to extremes they can be viable techniques for self-control."[1]

Repeated rituals can also have a soothing effect on one's nerves. In *The Bright Lights: A Theatre Life* actress Marian Seldes explained, "There is a ritual in the dressing room, private for some, gregarious for others. The look of the room, the temperature, where each article of clothing is set — yours and the character's — mementos from other plays. A different robe for the theater. Special towels, soap, cologne. Brushes and combs. The actual tubes or sticks of makeup."[2] Many elements and practices combine to produce this soothing pre-performance ritual.

You can create your own rituals and ceremonies out of these same sorts of elements and practices, setting up your writing space or your painting studio with objects that hold symbolic meaning for you, preparing yourself to write or paint in a certain ceremonial way (perhaps using the incantations described in chapter 11), and turning to your creative work in the context of the ceremonies and rituals you create for yourself. Your ritual ceremony might be as simple as lighting a candle or repeating an affirmation or as involved as creating a Japanese tea ceremony. Experiment and discover for yourself what rituals and ceremonies work for you to reduce your anxiety.

☑ TO DO

Create a list of ceremonies and rituals that might work to calm you. Look over the list. Pick out one or two rituals that resonate and feel most useful, and try them out in your mind's eye. If it seems as if they might prove effective, practice using them the next time you experience anxiety welling up.

CHAPTER 18

THE ANXIETY OF PERFORMING

Performance — which includes the act of coming to the blank page or the blank canvas, as well as standing up in front of an audience — is a classic anxiety producer. It is so potent an anxiety producer because it consists of a great many different fears: the fear of being seen as flawed, the fear of criticism, the fear of disappointing people, the fear of being in power, the fear of embarrassment and humiliation, the fear of imperfection, the fear of loss of control, and even more dramatic fears like the fear of loss of love and approval and the fear of annihilation. Performance anxiety is made up of such a long list of fears that it is no wonder so many people dread performing.

Mild performance anxiety is well-known to each of us. At such times we might experience butterflies in the stomach, the need to urinate, or a sense of disorientation. We are likely to react with more anxiety before important-seeming or difficult-feeling events, perhaps moving from butterflies to a feeling that approaches nausea or from slight disorientation to a feeling of dissociation. Each anxious person will have her own package of physical symptoms and distressing thoughts. As Stephanie Judy explained in *Making Music for the Joy of It*, "It's as if some Bad Fairy visits each [person] on concert day and bestows the most aggravating symptoms possible: a trembling arm to the strings, a dry mouth to singers, clammy hands to pianists, scant wind to the winds, and a foundering memory to us all."[1]

Psychological symptoms include feelings of confusion, disorientation, powerlessness, and loneliness. Some performers report briefly going deaf or blind. Additional psychological symptoms include the desire to escape or to hide, feelings of impending doom or death, or feelings of unreality. Opera singer Rosa Ponselle explained, "I actually prayed that a car would run me over so that I wouldn't have to die onstage — a prayer I was to repeat before every performance for the next twenty years." The soprano Ann Moffo recalled, "I've never started a performance without thinking, 'It's only the first act — I'll never live to see the final curtain.'" John Bonham, drummer for Led Zeppelin, admitted, "I've got terrible bad nerves all the time. Everybody in the band is the same and each of us has some little thing they do before we go on, like pacing about or lighting a cigarette."

The better a job you do of detaching from outcomes, getting a grip on your negative thoughts, and approaching life philosophically, the more likely it will be that you will be able to perform — in front of the blank canvas, in an interview situation, when networking, and in all the myriad situations in which a creative person performs — without experiencing anxiety. But no matter how mature or evolved you become, some amount of anxiety is likely to remain. In part this must be the case because our performances do matter to us, we do want to excel and represent ourselves well, and we have indeed made large investments of time, energy, and identity. Some anxiety will probably beset you, especially in those last few minutes and seconds before the performance commences, when performance anxiety is typically at its worst. Since anxiety is coming, make sure to practice your anxiety-management techniques and have a few proven techniques at the ready.

HEADLINE

Performance anxiety, because it is made up of so many pressing fears, afflicts almost everyone. You can probably only avoid it by not performing: by not writing, by not painting, by not networking, by not getting up onstage. Your best bet is to accept that it is coming and to prepare yourself.

☑ TO DO

Make sure you have at least one or two anxiety-management techniques in place to deal with performance anxiety Two of the best in this regard are discharge techniques (such as silently screaming) and reorienting techniques (in which you move your attention away from the performance). Choose your techniques, practice them, and make sure they work by using them in performance situations.

VOW

I will perform, even though performing makes me anxious.

ARI TEACHING TALE

The Singer Bedeviled by Anxiety

One day a young singer named Alice arrived at the shop behind which Ari kept his office. A tall woman in a white summer dress and a cream-colored shawl, she possessed an elegance that impressed Maya, with whom Alice chatted for a few minutes. Then it was time for Alice's appointment. She negotiated the narrow corridor rapidly, as if in a hurry to unburden herself.

"I don't know what it is," Alice began. Her hands twisted and untwisted. "I'm a singer. Here's the funny thing. The moment I step onstage, I'm perfectly calm. You might say that I'm in something like a profound trance once I begin singing. But beforehand I'm so anxious that I feel like I'm going to die. That anxiety bothers me so much that I've stopped altogether."

"I'm not following," Ari said mildly. "You're very anxious beforehand, but then you sing beautifully. What's the problem?"

Alice looked perplexed. "Well, all that horrible anxiety! There were times when I thought the anxiety would kill me!"

"You mean your stomach was all in knots, you had to run to the bathroom, you felt faint, you couldn't remember the lyrics, that sort of thing?"

"Yes! Exactly!"

"But only beforehand?"

"Yes!"

"Alice, there is no problem," Ari said after a moment.

He waited for his words to sink in. Alice, stunned, sat without speaking. Even her hands became still.

"Waiting is hell," Ari said. "So, while you wait, you are overcome by every manner of fear, doubt, and worry. A thousand nameless demons are whispering in your ear, telling you that you're about to fail. Your voice will crack. Your memory will desert you. People will boo and walk out. While you wait, you are the plaything of devils."

Alice nodded.

"You want to slay them?"

"Yes. Of course," she whispered.

"Then sharpen your sword. Be prepared by knowing your music, your intentions, and your soul. But I think you prepare exactly that way already."

"I thought that I might take some Inderal," Alice said after a moment. "If I ever decided to perform again."

"Some performers do take medicine," Ari agreed.

"You think I shouldn't?"

"I think no such thing."

Alice waited, expecting Ari to elaborate. But he didn't.

"You think I should?"

"I think no such thing."

Now tears sprang to her eyes. "I can't go on like this!" she cried. "My stage fright is incapacitating me!"

"Alice, you don't have stage fright. You are not frightened when you appear onstage. Are you?"

"No. Never!"

"You suffer from the anxiety of waiting and worrying. That's as different as night and day. It's the price you're paying for living the life you were destined to lead."

"I thought…there are all kinds of techniques…I thought that you could teach me some."

"Certainly. We can create a visualization for you. You can learn the Sarnoff Squeeze. You can learn a breathing technique. I can teach you a technique called confronting your symptoms. You could learn to silently scream. You could practice a battle cry. You could learn thought stopping and thought substitution. We could devise a mudra for you — that's the gesture the Buddha used to stop a rampaging elephant. Techniques are excellent things."

"I'd like to learn one or two of those," Alice replied in a whisper. "So I can feel armed."

"Of course. We'll equip you with one or two excellent techniques. But what's the most important thing?"

The singer thought. "That I accept this fear and sing anyway."

"That's your affirmation, Alice. It's perfect and beautiful. Repeat it."

"I accept this fear and sing anyway."

"Now sing for me."

Alice looked startled. "I couldn't. I have to warm up first. Sometimes it takes me twenty minutes —"

"Alice. Repeat your affirmation. Then sing me a lovely song."

Alice blinked. Her fear and distress registered in her face, her posture, and even in the way she held her hands.

"I accept fear and sing anyway," she said. A moment passed. "I accept fear and sing anyway," she repeated. She cleared her throat and began to sing. First she sang ever so softly. But then her voice began to ring out — so strongly and confidently that Maya, tending to a customer, thought to herself, "I believe he's turned on the radio! What a strange thing to do in the middle of a session!"

Alice's singing filled the bazaar and made everyone happy.

MORAL: Who doesn't fear performing? And, as a consequence, how much music is lost?

Your Anxiety Mastery Menu

HIGHLIGHTING: REORIENTING TECHNIQUES

What you focus on plays a large part in determining how much anxiety you feel. If, before a performance or a meeting with an editor, you focus on how important this event is for your career and on how unprepared you feel, you're pretty much bound to grow anxious. On the other hand, if you focus on the cherry bobbing in your Coke, you will have oriented yourself away from the impending event and will reduce your experience of anxiety. It can often be exactly this simple to reduce your anxiety, especially if you mindfully practice this technique: orient away from the source of anxiety and toward neutral stimuli.

In his book *Kicking the Fear Habit* Dr. Manuel Smith argues that each of us has a powerful "reorienting reflex" that we can effectively employ to manage our anxiety. He explains that we naturally orient to five kinds of stimuli: 1) "Stimuli with novelty: Anything that is unexpected or new"; 2) "Stimuli with biological significance: Anything that satisfies our biological hungers"; 3) "Stimuli with innate signal value: Anything that we instinctually orient to such as bodily sensations"; 4) "Stimuli with learned or acquired signal value: Anything that we have learned to pay attention to"; and 5) "Stimuli with instructed signal value: Anything that we have been told or instructed to pay attention to, either by others or ourselves."[2]

I ask my coaching clients to try their hand at learning and practicing reorienting. Liz, a doll maker, reported, "I was approaching my sewing table this morning when I asked myself, 'Where might I reorient my focus to take the attention off the work and help me slide into the work on this doll?' I decided that for today I would try thinking about the circus that I went to with my grandchildren last Friday. I found myself lightening up and smiling. I sat right down and worked on the arm that I was worried would be a problem. The arm turned out to be quite a challenge and I was right to be worried, but by reorienting I got straight to work rather than procrastinating and avoiding it."

The shorthand for what we're talking about is the question, "Where will I focus my attention?" You can focus on your worries, fears, doubts, and anxiety, or you can focus on something neutral, distracting, or positive. If you discover that you are having trouble orienting away from your fears and your worries, that likely means that you vigilantly hold your focus on the stimulus that is making you anxious, as a robbery victim might focus fixedly on the revolver the robber is pointing at him. You can't seem to take your eye off the stimulus because you perceive it as a grave threat. Therefore, you may have to add the following step to your reorienting practice: before you orient away from the stimulus that makes you anxious, say to yourself, "It's all right that I don't focus on my anxious feelings. Nothing bad will happen if I shift my focus away from those feelings." By gaining permission to look away, you can start using this simple but powerful technique.

☑ TO DO

Practice reorienting by bringing an anxious thought to mind and then seeing what sort of stimulus serves to move your mind from its fixation on that anxious thought. Try out different sorts of stimuli from the five categories that Smith describes: you might try reorienting to something else, from the aroma of your mint tea to a mantra you construct for yourself to a picture of someone attractive to you. Practice and learn this technique: It is simplicity itself once you master it.

CHAPTER 19

THE ANXIETY OF SELLING

In some cultures creativity is woven into the fabric of society, and singing, dancing, weaving, and potting are not done to sell but are part of community life. In most cultures, however, people who want to have a creative life working in a particular art discipline - - if they want to dance, paint, write, sing, or act as their career — must sell their wares in the highly competitive art marketplace. Creative people would prefer that it be otherwise, because they do not see themselves as competing with their fellow artists, because selling feels unseemly, because it is such hard and odd work, and because it robs them of too much time that they would prefer to spend creating. But you have no choice: if you've chosen a creative career, you must sell.

This selling provokes anxiety. One way to deal with this anxiety is simply not to enter the fray. This might sound like

"I paint for myself" or "I'll find someone else to do the selling" or "I don't care who reads my writing — I do it for the process." Some people do indeed create for themselves and do not need to enter the fray. But many people who say that they are creating only for themselves say that because the marketplace seems too daunting and anxiety provoking. You will have to decide what is true for you: if you have decided not to enter the marketplace with your wares, is that because you are truly creating for yourself or because the marketplace feels too complex, hostile, and frightening?

Even simple-seeming tasks such as creating an effective artist's statement or querying literary agents can produce so much anxiety that some artists just don't get the tasks done. More complicated tasks such as building the "right" website, making sense of the marketing side of social media, figuring out how to connect with potential advocates and customers, and competing for limited gallery space or publishing slots produce that amount of anxiety and more, causing the typical creative person to put selling far down her to-do list. To avoid the anxiety provoked by the marketplace, creative people spend less time and give less attention to their marketing efforts than they should — and they know it.

The answer is not to fantasize that someone will discover you, to put up a website and imagine that you have done enough to market yourself, or to otherwise avoid making a strong marketing effort. Rather, the answer is to expect anxiety and to deal with it. For some creative people nothing feels harder, more inscrutable, or scarier than dealing with the marketplace. Nevertheless, do everything in your power to make useful marketplace connections and advocate for your wares. This will most likely produce a lot of anxiety — but you are learning to manage it. Trust your anxiety-management skills, and use them in the service of your career.

HEADLINE

Most creative people find that selling provokes anxiety. If you are in this large category, opt for dealing with the anxiety rather than avoiding the marketplace.

☑ TO DO

Go over your anxiety mastery menu and think through how each of the strategies might work in the context of reducing your selling anxiety. If one or two stand out as possibilities, practice them and begin to use them in your marketplace dealings.

VOW

If I intend to have a career in the arts, I will not let anxiety stop me from marketing energetically.

PHOEBE TEACHING TALE

THE FROG AND THE BEE PROPOSE AN AMUSEMENT

On Sunday morning Phoebe slept in until nine. When she awoke she watched a little television, flipping from church shows to political shows to cooking shows and finally settling on a show for fishermen. The show had to do with the tricks you could employ during fly-fishing competitions to make your competitors think that you were catching a lot of fish. Phoebe watched because she was genuinely puzzled. It seemed much more important to actually catch some fish than to fool your competitors! The point of the program escaped her.

Just as the show ended and a commercial for lures began, the frog and the bee appeared. They were in high spirits. The frog hopped onto Phoebe's bed, and the bee quivered on the lip of Phoebe's crookneck desk lamp.

"Good morning!" said the frog.

"We have something to propose!" said the bee.

"We have planned an amusement for you today —"

"An a-muse-ment," the bee repeated, underlining the pun.

"Which we think you will really enjoy —"

"But only if you aren't too busy creating and such like —"

"Because a muse's prime directive is to never stop a creator from creating!"

Phoebe, her head on a swivel as the frog and the bee breathlessly interrupted each other, caught her breath.

"What is the amusement?" she asked. "Because I was going to work on my novel.... But I could also use an amusement, sixth grade being what it is."

"You decide," said the frog.

"We'll wait," said the bee.

"You haven't told what the amusement *is*!" Phoebe exclaimed petulantly. She was already upset at herself for choosing the amusement over her novel, which choice she recognized she was going to make if the amusement was at all interesting.

"At the town gallery they are holding a juried competition for pastels. We muses are doing our own judging before the human judges arrive. You could join us and see the work and eavesdrop on our decision-making process."

"What is it you decide?" Phoebe asked, not quite understanding.

"Why, which are the best!" the frog exclaimed.

She vaguely knew that there were juried art competitions where prizes were given out. In fact, she suddenly remembered that the main complaint of the early Impressionists was that they couldn't get their paintings into the major competitions of their day, the yearly salons, and so had to form their own antisalons as a way to give themselves prizes. So the idea of turning art into a horse race was hardly new. But what an idea! If there were fifteen great things at a show, or a hundred, and three prizes, what exactly was the point in making ninety-seven excellent things losers?

"Let's go!" Phoebe said. "I want to see this judging phenomenon, which I think is quite stupid."

The gallery was a spanking-new space off the main street of downtown. It was light, airy, high ceilinged, and divided into several ample-sized rooms in which artwork hung. The frog and the bee took Phoebe in a side entrance. There were thirty or so muses inside, all with very small pads and pens, moving about the pastels and making notes.

"We all judge," the frog said.

"Very democratic," the bee said.

"It's still stupid," Phoebe said. "Choosing winners and losers."

Phoebe wandered about. Most of the pastels were landscapes or other scenes from nature. She liked many of them and didn't like about an equal number. She especially liked one called *Deep Green Forest*. "This is the best one," she heard herself saying. Then she recoiled. "Did I just say that? How incredibly —" She didn't know what word to add and shook her head in dismay.

She moved on and stopped in front of a large pastel called *Gold Hills*, done by an artist named Frank Rankling. Seven or eight muses were gazing at it with rapt attention.

"Extraordinary line," said Melanie Caterpillar.

"Exceptional intensity," said Harold Spider.

"Amazing handling of light and shadow," said a gnat whom Phoebe didn't know.

"Much better than *Dark Green Forest* —" said a toad.

"Which was so somber —" said Melanie Caterpillar.

"Or *Three Red Ponies* —" said the gnat.

"Which was *so* Franz Marc!" said Harold Spider.

"Masterful use of cliché," said Phoebe, annoyed with the muses and their judging. "I mean, shouldn't your deliberations be kept secret? You're making it perfectly clear to each other that you really like this one. How can that not affect the ultimate judging?"

"We are completely independent when we judge," said the gnat.

"We remember nothing that we hear," said the toad.

"Whatever!" exclaimed Phoebe. She turned on her heels, leaving *Gold Hills* in the dust.

The funny thing was that the process of judging was making her dislike Frank Rankling, the painter of *Gold Hills*, and, really, why be mad at him? Suddenly she realized that winners, if they were at all ethical, should always accept their prizes diffidently and even a little sadly — even if they were simultaneously thrilled — on account of knowing that they were winning at someone else's expense.

She searched out the frog and the bee, who were relaxing on a counter where champagne was being served.

"What's the point of making this a competition?" Phoebe asked. "Why not just have a group show? Isn't that more humane and civilized?"

"It's Darwinian," replied the frog. "There must be winners and losers, or else museums would have to be as large as cities. Where would we keep everybody's unjudged art? Every bookstore would have to be as massive as the Smithsonian or the British Library. You'd need as many movie theaters as Burger Kings. And so on. Without judging — which of course isn't the same as good judgment! — the world would explode with undifferentiated stuff."

Phoebe was inclined to treat evolutionary theory with respect. She considered the frog's argument.

"But you agree that it's not fair?" she said, mulling the matter over.

"Agreed! No more fair than a spider eating a fly or a person eating a cow."

"But it's necessary," added the bee. "Otherwise the

world would become like a Dutch warehouse, where they store all the art that got made, because the Dutch government subsidized artists, that nobody now wants."

"Exactly!" exclaimed the frog. "Without competition the world would become a Dutch warehouse."

"It's terribly important that someone be number one, somebody be number two, and so on, or else —"

"I know!" Phoebe cried. "A Dutch warehouse!" With that she stomped away.

"Where are you going?" cried the frog.

"I'm going home," Phoebe said over her shoulder. "I do not like this one little bit."

As Phoebe walked home she thought about competition. She didn't like it; in fact, she hated it. But she understood what the frog and the bee were saying. It was, as the frog had said, Darwinian. It wasn't about right or wrong, good or bad. Some movie had to be number one. Some pop star had to be number one. Some painter had to be number one. The universe, by overpopulating itself, demanded it.

"Well, then, I will be number one," she suddenly exclaimed. "I will be very modest, very clear in my own mind that I am not special by virtue of having won. But I accept the shape of the universe. I would rather win the Nobel Prize for literature than not." She nodded her head. "A Dutch warehouse!" she cried. "Matter must be differentiated!" She wasn't positive that she believed the frog's evolutionary argument, but she was absolutely certain that she preferred winning to losing.

MORAL: There will always be judging. Get ready for it.

Your Anxiety Mastery Menu

HIGHLIGHTING: PREPARATION TECHNIQUES

You can reduce your anxiety by being well prepared for situations that provoke anxiety in you. If public speaking makes you anxious and you're about to give interviews and talks in support of your new book, preparing answers beforehand will help with the interviews, and preparing your bookstore chat will help with the book signings. A great deal of the anxiety we experience is anticipatory, and carefully preparing is the key to reducing this kind of anxiety.

Being prepared — for your next concert, for your upcoming meeting with a literary agent, for the interviews you do in support of your current film — reduces anxiety. Pianist and conductor Vladimir Ashkenazy reflected on how musicians can effectively manage performance anxiety: "Working hard at practice is also the best defense I know against pre-concert nervousness. That nervousness can never be entirely eliminated but it can be psychologically prepared for by convincing yourself that you have done all the homework necessary for a solid performance." Or as Spencer Tracy succinctly put it, "First of all, learn your lines."

Practice and rehearsal can be great anxiety reducers. This also means practicing techniques and strategies that help you present yourself more confidently and fearlessly and that reduce your anxiety, techniques such as the ones I've been describing. You will also want to mentally rehearse upcoming events or interactions that typically provoke anxiety in you. As Ann Seagrave put it in *Free from Fears*, "Imagery desensitization gives us an opportunity to think or imagine a situation the way we would like it to occur. Instead of imagining that a catastrophe will befall you, imagine that you will feel comfortable and secure in the situation. Rest assured that you will reach the point of being able to think through or imagine a feared situation without having an anxiety reaction."[1]

Research conducted by Donald Meichenbaum has shown how mental imaging can become a technique of great power and versatility. When you mentally rehearse, you provide yourself with the chance to practice your coping skills and anxiety-management techniques. You bring the impending event or situation to mind, notice your negative thoughts or anxiety reactions, and stop everything to try out a technique right then and there. Mental imaging provides you with the opportunity to work through anxiety-provoking situations in the privacy of your own mind.

Preparation is a large word and includes many sorts of activities, from really learning your lines to practicing how to speak about your novel to organizing your life so that there is room for the ambitious painting project you intend to begin. It means rehearsing; it means readying yourself for what is to come; it means identifying likely challenges and obstacles and knowing what you will do should they occur. Do you know what you will do if you start to doubt your current painting style, if you can't find the right word to finish your poem, or if you learn that your only published novel is going out of print? Know what you will do. Prepare yourself as best as you can for as much as you can. Doing so will forestall a lot of anxiety.

☑ TO DO

Try using mental rehearsing on an upcoming situation or event. When you're done, describe what you've learned from the experience.

CHAPTER 20

THE ANXIETY OF PROMOTING

Life is indeed Darwinian. You may not personally feel that you are competing with another creative person, and in fact you may feel nothing but kinship for your brother and sister creators. But you and your creative products are nevertheless competing with every other creative person's wares for the attention of buyers and for a foot in the marketplace. You know in your heart that self-promotion and product promotion are probably more important ingredients in the success of a song, novel, painting, or play than the quality of the product. This thought may sadden or anger you — but feeling upset won't make this reality go away.

You will need to promote what you do, which means giving interviews, speaking in front of audiences, building your social media presence, creating a fan base, making pitches to people who may be of help to you, and even engaging in stunts.

Consider just the first two of these, giving interviews and speaking in front of audiences. Since public speaking always tops any list of phobias, beating out spiders, bridges, and flying, it would be little wonder if the prospect of speaking on behalf of your creative efforts made you anxious. It makes almost everyone anxious!

Most likely the idea of promoting, as well as each actual promotional gambit, makes you anxious. That's a double whammy that you must learn to overcome. Every so often an artist gets away with not needing to promote his wares — his novel simply takes off, his paintings are simply wanted. More often, though, an artist's promotional energy and involvement make the difference between sales and anonymity. Maybe the gods of whimsy will smile on you and your wares will take off without your needing to promote them. But get ready for the more usual scenario, in which nothing much happens without advertising, publicity, and promotions. Jump into these waters — and use your anxiety-management tools to deal with any anxiety that accompanies your promotional efforts.

HEADLINE

Promotional tasks such as being interviewed, speaking in front of audiences, and making pitches to potential partners make most people anxious. Get ready for these tasks and get ready for the accompanying anxiety.

☑ TO DO

Picture yourself promoting yourself and your creative products. What do you see yourself doing? If you can't get a clear picture, presume that anxiety is getting in the way. Use one of your anxiety-management tools to calm yourself, and then try again to visualize promoting yourself and your creative products. Continue with this exercise until you have a clear, distinct vision of you promoting.

VOW

I will promote what I create. That is how I advocate for my work and have a career. If some anxiety accompanies my promotion efforts, I will deal with it.

ARI TEACHING TALE

PLASTER VOMIT FOR SALE

Ari accepted that every human being was a mass of contradictions. The shy exhibitionist, the lusty innocent, the foul-mouthed puritan, the cold-hearted martyr, the slovenly neat-freak — nothing surprised him. So it came as no surprise that Donald, the sculptor who sat across from him today, appeared both iron strong in his iconoclastic creating and weak-kneed about promoting his creations.

"I do plaster sculptures of vomit," the sculptor began. "About this size." He held his hands two feet apart. "Nobody buys them. I need to promote them. But I won't. Should I tell you why?" Donald was a small, sarcastic man looking for a fight.

Ari smiled. "No, thanks, I can imagine why. Just let me make sure that I understand you. You are brave, nonconforming, self-directing, and nose-thumbing enough to create plaster sculptures of vomit, but you are not brave, nonconforming, self-directing, and nose-thumbing enough to promote your plaster sculptures. That's about right, isn't it?"

"Not brave enough!" the sculptor exclaimed. "I should smack you one!"

"Promoting makes you anxious," Ari continued blandly. "I'm sure it's that simple..But why don't you explain it in your own way. I'm sure you have many explanations."

The sculptor leaped to his feet. "The heck with you! I'm leaving!"

Ari poured himself some tea. After a moment the sculptor sat back down.

"No, first I am going to explain myself," the sculptor announced. "Then I'll be leaving!"

"Fig?" Ari said, holding out the plate.

"Thank you," the sculptor replied.

Ari laughed. "That was very mild and mannerly of you!"

"You think I'm a lamb in wolf's clothing? Is that it? Let me tell you. Once I —"

Ari raised his hand. "We all have our war stories. Just explain to me why not promoting your sculptures is a matter of something other than anxiety."

The sculptor calmed himself, sat back, and thought.

"All right. I think there are eleven reasons why I —" He paused, looking for the right word.

"Refuse," Ari said.

"Am disinclined," the sculptor resumed. "Eleven reasons why I am disinclined to promote my work.

First, it's unseemly. I might as well be wearing a sandwich board or holding out a tin can for quarters. Second, it steals time from creating. Third, how do you describe art? It's ridiculous to try. Fourth, it's always who you know, not what efforts you make, and I know no one, so why bother? Fifth, capitalism and commercialism are vices, not virtues, and ruin the purity of art. Sixth, only silly, saccharine things sell, and so I might as well not bother trying to hawk serious things. Seventh, selling is not my skill set. Eighth, I am the worst salesman of my own work since I don't like people and only alien ate them. Ninth, people are dense and won't get what I'm trying to do, so why bother? Tenth, I have no track record of my work appreciating in value, and collectors are only interested in artists whose work appreciates, so I am a dead loss to them. Eleventh, selling sucks."

Ari clapped his hands enthusiastically. "What an excellent list!" he exclaimed. "That is an almost perfect list. No one could have done better!"

The sculptor waited for Ari to continue.

"And they are all red herrings," Ari finally said. "Excellent red herrings, beautiful red herrings, but all red herrings. I could tackle them one by one, but life is too short. Did you hear about the artist who took his paintings out back of his house and peppered them with buckshot? The video went viral. Three million people watched it."

"Even I watched it," the sculptor said sulkily.

"Made his name. He went on television. Now he's famous."

"Is *that* what you want me to do? I'd shoot myself first. Not my sculptures — me."

"You don't think that he had fun with that?" Ari asked, leaning forward. "You don't think that he is every bit as ironic and sarcastic as you are? You don't think he laughed all the way to the bank?"

The sculptor pondered that. "I suspect that he's got a deep well of irony and sarcasm," he agreed after a moment. "So I should pull some stunt?"

Ari shrugged.

"What sort of stunt did you have in mind?" the sculptor asked. There was no masking his genuine curiosity.

"Me?" Ari dropped back in his seat. "I could dream up a hundred stunts in a minute flat. Drop your plaster vomit sculptures into an empty field from a plane. Send the president a plaster vomit sculpture and get outraged when the White House won't accept it. Crash an A-list party and bring plaster vomit sculptures to distribute to the alcoholic actors and actresses in attendance. Dreaming up stunts is a snap! You could dream up a million. Couldn't you?"

"I suppose," the sculptor replied truculently. "I can't quite get my mind to think that way."

Ari smiled. "No, your mind is racing now, thinking about stunts. I can tell. Can you feel how suddenly you're not anxious? Can you feel the difference?"

The sculptor blinked. Ari watched him process his

internal state. He thought long and hard, occasionally nodding.

"I am less anxious," he said. "More like fired up than anxious. So I'm supposed to dream up some stunt?"

"Forget about stunts!" Ari exclaimed. "That was a stunt, bringing up stunts! What I want you to discern is how different it feels getting excited about promoting your work and getting anxious about promoting your work. For a minute there you got excited. You're still excited. Aren't you?"

The sculptor wasn't listening. Suddenly he said, "You know, I have a stunt in mind. I'm going to get an elephant, and some confederates, and walk the elephant through town, and then every time the elephant drops a turd a confederate will run out into the street and substitute one of my sculptures for the elephant's turd. How about that?"

"That's pretty far-out," Ari said, smiling. "Make sure to get some good video."

"Then I can let the elephant loose and have him trample some gallery owners, maybe a collector or two, and a curator."

"Donald —"

"Just kidding!" He stopped suddenly. "All this not promoting, all these years — decades now — of not promoting, that was just anxiety?"

"Yes," Ari said quietly. "Just some wispy, diffuse anxiety. Nothing gigantic — just enough to make it easy for you to throw up your hands and skip the effort."

"Wow," the sculptor said, shaking his head. "I feel like an idiot."

Ari smiled. "Have a fig. And some tea. And tomorrow —"

"And tomorrow," the sculptor exclaimed, "maybe I'm not renting an elephant, but I am definitely doing something!"

MORAL: Nature requires self-promotion. Why else would butterflies be so colorful?

Your Anxiety Mastery Menu

HIGHLIGHTING: SYMPTOM CONFRONTATION TECHNIQUES

Symptom confrontation is a technique associated with existential psychotherapy and with the therapists Milton Erickson and Viktor Frankl in particular. In therapy of this sort a client is commanded, apparently paradoxically, to do more of the thing that he came into therapy wanting to do less of. Trying to increase your symptoms in order to make them disappear is a technique that may or may not appeal to you. More queasiness? More woolly-headedness? More palpitations? What an idea! But if the idea intrigues you, by all means investigate it.

In her book *A Soprano on Her Head*, Eloise Ristad, an advocate of this technique who used it in her performance anxiety workshops, explained: "Take one of your own symptoms — clammy hands, shaky knees, or whatever — and apply the... principle of pushing it to the point where it can go no further. Do *not* try to control it or make it go away; try only to increase the intensity and see how far you can carry this particular symptom....If you are like most people, you will find you can't push your symptom past a certain point, and that when you reach that point the symptom actually reverses.... You may find that almost as soon as you *try* to intensify a symptom, it begins to disappear."[1]

Not only can you confront the symptoms you have, you can create symptoms you don't have. Are you only suffering from butterflies in your stomach? Why not have your palms sweat too? Indeed, why not worry about worrying? — an exercise know as "transcendental metaworry." As Frankl put it, "A sound sense of humor is inherent in this technique.... Humor helps man rise above his own predicament by allowing him to look at himself in a more detached way."[2]

But Frankl is quick to point out that his "paradoxical intention" technique is not a superficial one, even if it employs humor: "I am convinced that paradoxical intention...enables the patient to perform on a deeper level a radical change of attitude, and a wholesome one at that."[3] If you find this technique a congenial one, if you practice it, and if you add it to your arsenal of anxiety-management techniques, you may be surprised to discover what an effective job it does of not only reducing your anxiety symptoms but of ridding them entirely.

☑ TO DO

In your mind's eye, try confronting a physical symptom like sweaty palms or wobbly knees or a mental symptom like your inability to concentrate or your sense of impending doom. Can you see how this technique might work with physical and mental symptoms? Do you sense that it might work for you? If you do, use it when an actual mental or physical symptom presents itself.

CHAPTER 21

THE ANXIETY OF PROCRASTINATING

Procrastination is an anxiety state. Maybe we are not getting to our creative work for one of the reasons discussed in these lessons. But then, as we stall and procrastinate, the procrastination itself produces more anxiety. Days, weeks, and months vanish as we remain immobilized. It's as if we're held in check by invisible bonds; and the anxiety that arises is akin to the anxiety we'd experience if we were imprisoned and desperately hoping to escape. We feel trapped by our resistance and unequal to freeing ourselves, even though we know that the door to our prison has no lock.

We know that the prison door has no lock, and this certain knowledge starts to erode our self-image and produce endless negative self-talk. Why don't we just *do* it? What are we waiting for? Why are we so weak, undisciplined, and cowardly?

How can we possibly let everyday chores and errands obliterate our creative work? How can we look at ourselves in the mirror? How can we tell the people who are counting on us that we are hiding out and getting nothing done? A mountain of a problem has replaced whatever initially caused us to block — some difficulty in the third chapter of our novel or a little trouble with that red spot in a corner of the painting. Now we're confronted by the anxiety of procrastination and our eroding self-image.

This becomes a classic vicious cycle, in which our new anxiety prevents us from dealing with whatever provoked our initial anxiety and caused us to procrastinate. Now we must really bring our anxiety-management tools to the fore! We need to discharge the stress, breathe, deal with our inflamed cognitions, and use every method in our arsenal to reduce our anxiety so that we can get back to work. Everyone knows how procrastination can end in an instant: for a month we were resistant to writing that boring term paper and now that the deadline is tomorrow the door swings open and we escape into work. Remember that a bout of procrastination can end instantly if you bring your anxiety-management skills to bear on it.

HEADLINE

Anxiety causes procrastination, and procrastination produces more anxiety. Get out of this vicious cycle by recognizing how much anxiety is at play and by employing your very best anxiety-management tools to interrupt — and end — the cycle.

☑ TO DO

Decide what will constitute procrastination — two days of not creating, three days of not creating, four days of not creating? — and make a pact with yourself that when you hit that number you will announce that you are stalled and take immediate action to get yourself working again.

VOW

If I've stopped working and started procrastinating, I will forthrightly address my stalled state.

PHOEBE TEACHING TALE

THE INTERNATIONAL CONFERENCE OF MUSES

Phoebe was perturbed by her lack of muses. They hadn't visited for three or four days, and she was missing them.

Of course, it wasn't really clear what work, if any, muses did, or what benefits, if any, muses conferred. Still, she missed them. None had visited in what seemed like the longest time, and somehow that connected to her not being able to begin her odious history paper.

She missed Harold Spider in particular. Normally he would arrive, engage Phoebe in conversation, and ask how she was doing or if anything was bothering her. She, in turn, would ask him what he thought about her choice for a science project or an English essay. It was true that to her request for advice Harold would invariably reply, "What do you think?" or "What are your choices?" or "Which way are you leaning?" But even those sidestepping questions would coax her into a further explanation of her situation, which was a good thing. And sometimes Harold Spider would ask a really provocative question, which was even better. This coaxing or coaching had been going on for a long time; now, for days, nothing.

Phoebe wondered if the muses were away on vacation or perhaps at a conference. Where were they? Would her big history paper, which was due on Friday and which, by virtue of its incredibly boring nature, she had not yet begun, be doomed by their absence? She knew that the best answer was simply to start, muse or no muse, but she found herself saying, "As soon as a muse appears, I will begin! Best not to start without a muse in sight!"

Phoebe was quite interested in the gypsies of Central Europe and the atomic bombing of Japan. About those subjects she could have read volumes and written happily. But the subject of her eight-page paper was the yawn-producing "Western expansion of the 1840s." Golly! People left the East and headed to the West. What could be simpler to understand? You ran up a debt, and to avoid debtors' prison you joined a wagon train. You woke up one morning, looked at your wife, and set off on horseback. What more was there to say?

Certainly each traveler had his or her own story. But basically it was so simple and obvious! It seemed a crime — child abuse! — to have to write eight long pages on something as transparent as why people would move from one place to another. Wasn't it enough to say, "They had their reasons"? Couldn't she just make a bulleted list — eight pages, she calculated, would come to two hundred bullets — of why people would head west? Bullet one: to grab some land. Bullet two: for adventure. Bullet three: to avoid the law. And so on.

But Mr. Teasdale would not have accepted a bulleted list, not in a million years. So Phoebe remained stuck, having to research this transparent subject and say in well-formed paragraphs the most obvious things.

It was Wednesday, and it was getting harrowing. Oddly enough, she found herself getting angry with the muses. "I need a muse!" she heard herself saying. "Where are they? What can they be doing?" She knew it was unreasonable to be furious with the muses, since they offered so little help when they did appear, and since, to be completely honest about it, she wasn't at all sure they were muses. I mean, would you believe a bug? So it was silly to put so much stock in these little self-proclaimed muses. Still, she found herself getting angrier and angrier.

At school on Wednesday everybody in Mr. Teasdale's class was complaining about the paper. Nobody, it appeared, had begun it. A few claimed that they would never begin it. Mass rebellion or mass procrastination had hit Mr. Teasdale's students. This did nothing to cheer Phoebe, who knew that she would have to write the paper no matter what anybody else did. Where were those darned muses?

Matters came to a head when she got home. She had only tonight and Thursday night to write eight long pages. Plus, she couldn't just write; she had to read. She had eleven books out from the library on the various westward expansion themes, and they stood in a tall, re-proachful pile in the middle of her room, surmounted by Lexington the cat, who had gotten in the habit of leaping back and forth from her worktable to the book pile.

Four o'clock came and went. Four thirty did the same. Soon it was four fifty. Golly! She had actually forgotten about muses and was simply in a panic. She pummeled her forehead a few times, ran downstairs for a cookie, grabbed two, trotted back upstairs, put on her headphones, and played several rock anthems. Then she shut her eyes tight and bit the bullet.

"All right!" she cried out loud. "I will write this thing!"

She grabbed a piece of paper. "Eight pages," she wrote. "A one-page introduction, I should think. And a one-page conclusion. So, six pages of middle. Should that be six pages at one reason each or twelve half-page reasons? Well, I suppose I need to know how many good reasons there are." She hopped up, knocked Lexington off the books, sat down on the carpet, and circled the books around her. "Circling the wagons!" she murmured. She attacked the books with single-minded determination. She moved from book to book culling headlines and highlights. Within twenty minutes she had a list of eight reasons.

"Eight," she said. "Well, that's awkward. But all right!"

She began writing her paper in longhand. "There

were at least eight important reasons for the westward expansion that took place during the 1840s. In this paper I will identify those reasons and explain why I think some were more important than others...."

A wild hour ensued. Phoebe whirled through her library books, jotted notes, copied out compelling quotes, arranged and rearranged her reasons until she was satisfied that they made at least superficial sense. Every so often she felt a tendril of satisfaction. Equally often she felt a tinge of residual anger. "Well, I will never wait for a muse again!" she cried. "They are simply unreliable!" Having gotten that off her chest, she resumed her wild creating.

As soon as she finished her paper, a great tumult arose. Many muses arrived, some carrying suitcases.

"We're just back from Paris!" Harold Spider exclaimed. "We had an excellent International Conference of Muses! The best workshops! A well-known Black Widow gave a splendid talk on creativity and destructiveness. And Leonard Fly came! You know, flies live for only one day. That makes fly muses, who live much longer but have a genetic remembrance of that short life, energetic, top-notch speakers. He gave the keynote address on Creativity in the Twenty-first Century. We networked, compared notes, and learned who's creating what in Japan and India and Fort Worth. A nice time was had by all!"

"I bet you skipped the workshops and ate far too many croque-monsieurs!" Phoebe replied petulantly.

"You are a *most* cynical young lady."

"Well, you could have told me! I had a horrible time with my history paper!"

"What? Did it not get done?" Harold Spider said mischievously.

"It got done! But I waited and waited for a muse to show up. Finally I couldn't wait any longer and I had to write it all in a rush. It was very unpleasant!"

"Well, next time I'll let you know when we're off to a conference," Harold Spider replied slyly. "Would that be better?"

"Oh, whatever!" Phoebe exclaimed. She knew what was going on. The muses were pulling her leg and providing another object lesson. They wanted to make it perfectly clear for the millionth time that you had to go merrily about your creating, muse or no muse. She got the message! She made every effort to ignore the muses scurrying about and nonchalantly finished her Pink Lemonade Snapple.

MORAL: You can wait to get started. But for how long? And to what purpose?

Your Anxiety Mastery Menu

HIGHLIGHTING: DISCHARGE TECHNIQUES

Stress builds up in the body, and doing something physical can release that stress. This physical action can be as simple as raising your arm and gesturing in a certain way. In *Raise Your Right Hand Against Fear*, psychotherapist Sheldon Kopp describes the Buddhist symbolic gesture known as a mudra: "Determined to destroy the Buddha, a dark and treacherous demon unleashed an elephant charging drunkenly. Just as the raging beast was about to trample him, the Buddha raised his right hand with fingers close together and open palm facing the oncoming animal. The fearless gesture stopped the elephant in its tracks and completely subdued the recklessly dangerous creature."[1] A gesture like a mudra, performed with power and intention, can send stress rocketing out of your body.

Other discharge techniques include shaking a fist or uttering a battle cry. You can create your own battle cry and treat the moment, whether you are in front of a blank canvas or preparing to meet with a gallery owner, as if you were a great hero. Imagine yourself as Don Quixote setting off on a magnificent quest, jousting with windmills, and shout "Charge!" as playfully and as wildly as you dare. You can discharge tension and stress by acting as if you are preparing for battle and by engaging in physical actions associated with battle, like real martial arts movements that you perform seriously or parodies of martial arts movements that you perform humorously.

Just moving about helps. You can pace, skip up and down, jog in place, stretch, or do a little walking meditation or yoga. You can go outside and walk or run around the block several times. Indeed, getting out can help significantly because sometimes what causes our anxiety is a sense of "inhibited flight" — that we are trapped in our studio with our painting or with our novel. Getting outside releases that anxiety as we prove to ourselves that we aren't really trapped. Remember to move — getting up and discharging tension physically is a better bet than sitting, brooding, and growing anxious.

Discharge techniques come in every shape and size. Dream

up some gesture or action — a wild dance, an amazing leap, a left jab followed by a right cross — that really works to release tension from your body and your mind. You might make zany faces, laugh out loud, or at least smile a little. The very act of smiling dissipates tension. If you can't make yourself smile just by ordering yourself to, then try telling yourself a good joke. Remember the basic principle: tension builds up in the body, and one of the best ways to get rid of that tension is to do something physical. Whether it's chopping wood or pirouetting across the room, use physicality to counteract the buildup of stress and anxiety.

☑ TO DO

Generate your own list of potential discharge techniques, look your list over, and choose one technique to practice. After you've practiced it a bit and tried implementing it when you feel anxious, evaluate whether you think you might like to add it to your anxiety-management tool kit.

CHAPTER 22

THE ANXIETY OF WAITING

reative people wait. We wait as we put our wares into the marketplace and wait for a literary agent, club owner, or gallery owner to say yes. We wait as a project incubates — even as we are working on this story, we know that we are really waiting on that story, the one we truly want to write but that isn't available to us yet. Even as we work to get it, we wait for our next acting opportunity, our next screenwriting opportunity, the next chance to get our symphony heard, the next chance to get our performance piece performed, the next chance to get our installation installed. We are active, busy, maybe too busy — and also waiting, waiting, waiting.

Waiting is remarkably taxing and provokes a lot of anxiety. A literary agent, the first to express any interest in your first novel, tells you that she'll get back to you in a few days, and now weeks have passed. What are you thinking? Probably something like the following: "Has she gotten to it yet? Does she hate it? Is she about to call and say she loves it? Will she ever get back in touch? Did she somehow lose my contact information? Should I send her a little email? Or will that irritate her? But what if she *did* lose my contact information and she's dying to get in touch with me? But that's silly — she could find my email address instantly by Googling me. So probably she hates it. Unless she hasn't gotten to it yet —" and so on.

Your best way to deal with all this waiting is a cognitive one in which you get a good grip on your mind by noticing your unhelpful and unnecessary inner chatter, disputing all that noise and unhelpfulness, and substituting soothing, sensible cognitions such as "I'll check in with her in two weeks — until then, I have no reason to give her a thought" and "These two weeks make for a perfect opportunity to get on with my new novel!" If, after you've done your excellent cognitive work, some tendril of anxiety remains, deal with it using one of the techniques you are beginning to master.

HEADLINE

Waiting is surprisingly taxing and produces more anxiety than you might imagine. Remember to keep busy, get a grip on your mind, and deal with any anxiety that remains.

☑ TO DO

Sit down and describe for yourself what tactics you will use whenever you find yourself waiting, whether for a job opportunity, a response from a marketplace player, or an idea to arrive. List the different sorts of waiting you will have to endure, what you will do in each case, and what anxiety-management tool you will employ in case anxiety wells up as you wait.

VOW

I acknowledge the reality that waiting is a regular feature of the creative process and the creative life, and I will learn ways to make waiting less oppressive and nerve-racking.

PHOEBE TEACHING TALE

The Frog and the Bee Nearly Come to Blows

The first week of spring passed uneventfully. Saturday morning dawned, and Phoebe discovered that she had a lot on her mind. A few days before she had begun wondering why the eye should consider blue and yellow complementary colors, which had caused her to start reading Newton, of all people. She associated Newton with gravity, but she came to learn that he was also "the father of optics" and, like Phoebe, extremely interested in color wheels.

She also learned that Newton was an odd duck. This had caused her mind to wander from optics to madness and, as a consequence, she had begun skimming Newton biographies. This landed her on a book by Julian Lieb and D. Jablow Hershman called *Manic Depression and Creativity*, one of whose subjects was Sir Isaac. What they wrote about Newton made her shake her head. They adduced his mania from behaviors that didn't sound so pathological, like running for Parliament and promoting the careers of young mathematicians (a behavior the authors called "the generosity of the manic").[1] How strange!

Something about all this didn't make sense to Phoebe

and, feeling intensely restless, she went to her favorite café and ordered her customary hot chocolate, her brain filled with odd and random thoughts — about Newton's fight with Leibnitz over the authorship of calculus, about whether flavored Fig Newtons were really Fig Newtons at all, and so on — and wandered out back to the patio, where it was bright and quiet.

The patio was mostly empty, and she could have sat by herself, but, being a writer (among other things), she preferred to sit near other beings and eavesdrop. She chose to sit next to the frog and the bee, two muses of her acquaintance. Although they were being quite loud and quarrelsome at the moment, which put Phoebe off, their animation piqued her interest. She smiled as she sat down, but they took no notice and continued their grumbling.

"Art for art's sake!" the frog was bellowing. "To quote Faulkner, a great poem is worth the lives of any number of little old ladies. And Picasso — didn't he claim that if he ran out of firewood for his kiln he would throw his wife and children in?"

"That's ridiculous!" screamed the bee. "Just what you'd expect from an alcoholic like Faulkner and an entertainer like Picasso! Art is for the sake of *people*, not itself. For the sake of the art maker, his daughter, the eleven people who read his poem, maybe even the executor of his estate who comes upon it after he is dead. But it can't be for its own sake! It doesn't *have* a sake, for Gosh sake!"

"You want art to have utility! Art exists! It just is! It mustn't serve any purpose!"

"You are one stupid academic frog who has lived too long in muddy water!" the bee buzzed, loud enough to scare a couple right off the terrace.

Phoebe couldn't help herself. "Excuse me," she said. "Would you call what you are having a philosophical discussion? I've thought about studying philosophy in college, and I'm curious if this is an example of what I might learn."

"I would call what we are doing fighting," the bee replied.

"Well," said Phoebe, gathering herself. "This strikes me as the biggest waste of time two muses could ever dream up. Is this an object lesson for me about how not to live? Did you know that I would be coming here for a Saturday hot chocolate and stage this conversation for my benefit?"

"Little girl, we have this fight every day of our lives! This is what we do," exclaimed the frog.

"And I have made thirty-three more excellent points than this nitwit frog and am currently ahead 982 to 949. At least. When I reach a thousand —"

"That is entirely wrong!" cried the frog. "Absolutely incorrect! I am ahead 961 to 709!"

Phoebe shook her head. There had to be a way of talking about creating that wasn't as silly as this!

"I have another point!" cried the frog. "The *best* point! If you look at art from a Taoist perspective —"

"Not the Taoist tactic! I won't permit it! I will sting you first."

The frog puffed up to twice its size, and the bee buzzed like a smoke detector. This was probably the way gods on Mount Olympus squabbled, Phoebe guessed, finally frying each other with lightning bolts and drowning each other in tsunami tidal waves. How silly of muses and gods!

"I have a question," Phoebe shouted above the din. "Shouldn't you be helping an artist, not fighting?"

This question seemed to thoroughly perplex the warring muses, who scrunched up their faces into serious frowns.

"What do you mean?" croaked the frog.

"What are you implying?" buzzed the bee.

"Well, take Shostakovich," Phoebe replied. "During World War Two he wrote several war symphonies. Each has a remarkable story, remarkable in the way that Shostakovich butted heads with his putative patron Stalin, remarkable in the way that he gathered musicians in the middle of such unbelievable hardship so that concerts could be performed, remarkable in the way that starving and homeless people came and filled concert halls to listen to his symphonies, remarkable in the way that his music unified and helped so many Russians in the middle of a terrible war. It seems to me that that is what an artist is for, and I just wonder why you aren't helping some artist somewhere who is trying to do some good work like that?"

There was a long silence.

"Ridiculous!" the frog finally exclaimed.

"Stupendously ignorant!" agreed the bee.

Phoebe sat stunned. She was sure that she had said something true and beautiful. Their reaction was incredible!

"But why not?" she cried, close to stamping her foot.

"You haven't asked the right question," said the frog. "Therefore it is pointless to try to answer."

"Plus," added the bee, "activism is such a tired idea! If you won't take the postmodern into account, there is just no hope for you!"

Phoebe turned back to her hot chocolate. "Well," she muttered, "who knew how disappointing muses could be." She concentrated in draining her drink past the dregs. Finally there was nothing to do but to go.

"I am leaving," she said. "Good day to you!"

She turned away quickly. Therefore she didn't notice that the frog and the bee were stifling smiles. When she was out of earshot, the frog spoke first.

"Very effective! Good work, bee. We did her a real service this morning."

"Excellent work, frog. I liked the Taoist reference. Nice touch!"

"Tremendous point she made about Shostakovich. Lovely. I almost started to cry."

As she walked home, Phoebe thought about self-reliance. She had the feeling that there was a Thoreau essay on the subject…or was it Emerson? At any rate, the point was indisputable. If you were going to write great symphonies in the middle of a world war and stand up to Stalin and make people a little happier with your music and all that, you couldn't wait for a frog or a bee to come inspire you. Certainly not *that* frog or *that* bee. Phoebe declared that when it came to creating, there was just no substitute for a person taking personal responsibility.

MORAL: Create as you wait. That way, as you will always be waiting, you will always be creating!

Your Anxiety Mastery Menu

Highlighting: Pharmaceuticals

Taking antianxiety medication is an option with some pluses and many minuses. The plus is that a chemical tranquilizer, if it works for you, will create an induced experience of calm. That state of calm can provide you with a crucial respite from your anxiety and allow you to begin trying nonchemical solutions that you might not have felt equal to trying while highly anxious. Among the minuses are the side effects of chemicals, the potential for dependency, and the way they divert us from looking for better solutions.

If your anxiety were in fact the result of some actual biological malfunction, as opposed to a completely natural reaction to perceived threats, it would certainly be sensible to put chemical relief on the table as one answer or even as the answer. But is anxiety usually an actual biological malfunction of some sort? It if isn't, then the chemical relief you receive is not a treatment for a biological disorder but just a medical tranquilizer.

In the first case the chemical is working because it is an appropriate treatment for a biological problem. In the second it is working because chemicals surely do things to people. Just think of speed, ecstasy, LSD, or magic mushrooms. Drugs can surely have effects. There is a fundamental difference between taking a drug because it is the answer to a biological problem and taking a drug because it can have an effect. This core distinction tends to be lost in the world of treating anxiety.

The magical leap that is customarily made from "we don't really know what you have" to "take a drug" naturally confuses smart, sensible people like you, who are not informed enough to ask this pertinent question: "Are you prescribing this drug because I have a biological problem, or are you prescribing this drug because it is known to rid me of symptoms?" A truthful doctor will answer, "The latter." Then you have a much better sense of where you stand.

But isn't ridding you of symptoms enough? If a painkiller rids you of pain, do you really care what is causing the pain? The answer is, Not always, but certainly sometimes. If the pain is from some innocuous mishap — say from a mildly pulled muscle — you do not need much except not to experience the pain. But what if the pain is caused by an ailment that really ought to be treated? Is chemically masking the pain a good answer in those circumstances? Not really.

The same is true with anxiety. Sometimes it makes sense to rid yourself of the symptoms of anxiety without endeavoring to find out what is causing those symptoms. But just as often you need to know *why* you are anxious, so that you can make changes that fundamentally improve your situation. I hope this distinction is clear to you and that, if you opt for pharmaceuticals, you nevertheless remember that you have work to do ridding yourself of anxiety in a more fundamental way.

☑ TO DO

Prescription medication is certainly an option. But informing yourself about the pros and cons of this option before choosing it is certainly wise.

CHAPTER 23

THE ANXIETY OF REPEATING

Creative people must do everything that they do — engage with the creative process, survive the rigors of the creative life, produce new excellent work, back up that work in the marketplace, and so on — over and over again, for an entire lifetime.

There is no guarantee that writing your fifth novel will produce any less anxiety than writing your first novel did. Indeed, we can imagine why it might actually produce more. First, you may be anxious about whether you have anything more to say. Second, you may be anxious about how to integrate the countless pieces of feedback you've gotten over the years (that you rely too heavily on dialogue, that your novels slog in the middle, and so on). Third, you may be anxious that people now count on your success in a way that they didn't in the beginning. And so on. Not only doesn't your fifth novel come with any guarantees, but it may well come with more pressure than did your first.

What if you've been lucky enough to have a large success? Then you find yourself in what will look like an enviable position to any artist who hasn't achieved success but that, in your shoes, only feels like an even more pressure-packed situation than before. You'll feel the pressure to strike while the iron is hot, so as not to miss your golden moment, the pressure to both surpass yourself and repeat yourself, so that your audience gets what it wants but also gets something "new and improved," and the pressure of dealing with a whole new cast of characters — fans, sycophants, wheeler-dealers, good-time Janes and Charlies. Success may be sweet, but it is not stress free.

You will have to repeat the process of engaging with your work and creating new work, and you will have to face the challenges that typically never go away: the occasional blues, the doubts about your talent, the dry spells and manic times, the books going out of print and the shows being canceled, the times you pay too much attention to your work and neglect your loved ones, and the times you neglect your creative work. It all happens again and again: and with it all comes the anxiety. As a seventy-year-old successful writer you will still get your rejection letters: Pearl Buck did, even after winning the Nobel Prize for Literature. There is no doubt about it: anxiety is on the way. Get your anxiety-management tools oiled and ready.

HEADLINE

A time never comes when life is settled and anxiety is banished. This is true for life in general, and triply true for the creative life.

☑ TO DO

Practice your anxiety-management skills in real-world situations. The sooner you actually practice them, the sooner you'll master them and be ready to use them when life — and anxiety — repeats itself.

VOW

I accept that the creative process and the creative life will always be challenging — and vow that I will try to bravely meet each new challenge.

ARI TEACHING TALE

THE FAMOUS ROCK BAND ON THE VERGE OF COLLAPSE

One day a whole rock band arrived at Maya's shop. The band was very famous and caused a great stir in the bazaar. Maya had to sternly remind the gathering crowd to be quiet and respectful.

The band milled about the shop, since Ari wasn't ready to see them yet. The leader of the band apologized to Maya for making the appointment on such short notice. They had been in the nearby city on tour and had decided on the spur of the moment to come to the oasis for help, which they sorely needed, he said. Maya replied that no apology was necessary and that Ari would be with them shortly.

After checking with her father in the back, Maya let the band know that Ari was ready to see them. One by one the band members traversed the narrow hall and entered the consulting room, which was dark and cool and had its back door open to the little, lemon-scented garden.

"Sit. Please," said Ari.

There were five of them, all male, all young, all lean, all intense looking.

"My name is Brian," the man in the middle said. "We're the Lime Death Squad. You've heard of us?"

Ari smiled. "No. I'm sorry."

"No matter! Just as well. We're having an incredibly terrible tour. Jason (here he nodded at a redhead who looked twisted up in pain) got sick and needed an emergency operation. Andy (here he nodded at a sullen, violent-looking young man), well, Andy will have to speak for himself. Mike (here he nodded at a young man who actually smiled when introduced) just got married and misses his wife and baby daughter and is constantly bitching about being away from them. Moses (here he nodded at a young man who looked like a soldier in the devil's brigade) can't think about anything but sex and is always bringing two or three girls around and doing it in our faces night and day. I write the songs, and I haven't had a good idea in about two years. It's all hit the fan on this tour, and if we don't kill each other it'll be a bloody miracle."

Ari nodded and turned to Andy, the angry one. "What drugs do you use?" he asked in a mild but direct way.

"Hey," Andy growled.

"Don't worry. I have a terrible memory. I won't remember what you tell me."

"Yeah, right. I use a little of this and a little of that. But I didn't come for a lecture!"

"Crack cocaine, meth, alcohol, marijuana," Brian said. "If you can ingest it, Andy will do it."

"Screw you," Andy replied.

Ari nodded. He turned to Moses the rake. "Why don't you write some songs? Don't you have songs in you?"

Moses made a face. "That's not my talent, man. I like to stand off to the side and watch the girls."

"So, Brian. You're the glue? You hold everything together?"

"I suppose. Though I've about had it!"

Ari grew very quiet and searched each man's face in turn.

"What's your question?" he finally said, addressing them all. "I don't cast spells. I don't break spells. What do you want from me? You look to be a rock band on the road, in the middle of a long tour, plagued by stardom, plagued by the traveling blues, plagued by your own personalities, plagued by too much time together and too much time on your hands, with a ready inclination to get high and all the other usual problems. What's new?"

No one replied. Then Mike, the man with the new wife and daughter, broke the silence.

"We used to enjoy ourselves more," he said. "We used to have fun. We were lighthearted Now everything feels dark and unmanageable. Something has changed.

Five years ago we rode in a van and were happy. Now we take over a whole floor of some great hotel, we get whatever we want, and we're miserable."

Ari nodded. "You had a dream, to become rock stars, and you achieved it. Then you came up against a meaning crisis, which you are now in the middle of. You are without meaning. So you fall back on old, second-rate meanings. Andy does drugs, which is a happy bondage. He also has his rage, which always comes in handy. Moses does sex, another happy way. You, you tried relationships, which might be a good solution if you happened to be with your loved ones, but you aren't. Brian creates, but he's not creating, so he has no meaning except the playing, which is old and stale. Jason, you carry the pain and tension of the whole band and even the whole world in your body and make yourself sick. The group meaning died. The simple, beautiful dream of becoming a famous rock band vanished by coming true. You got what you wished for, which is an excellent thing, but it left you bereft of meaning."

The band remained silent. Then Brian spoke. "That feels exactly right," he said. "We play our old songs, we work very hard on stage, we take pride in our performance, but it feels utterly meaningless."

"There are five things you must do," Ari said. "First, you have to help others. That is the best — sometimes the only — road to recovering meaning. You might meet with the Mothers of Charity in the city in which you now find yourself. They are very pious, bad-tempered women who minister to thousands of our country's saddest, sickest people. You could give them a million dollars, and your tour would improve instantly. Second, each of you must fall in love with two things. You all loved music once upon a time. You must fall in love with music again. And you must love a real person. Third, you must grow up, which means doing battle with your own disinclination to change. Fourth, you must respect how far you have come and do honor to the band. Fifth, each of you must create. Not just you, Brian, but all of you, because creativity is a path to life. Each of you must go deep and provide personal music for your next album. Each of you must contribute like an artist and a hero. If you do these five things, you can survive. If you don't, the band will break up."

They had only scheduled a ninety-minute appointment. But the band stayed for three hours. Ari worked with them as a group and as individuals, prying, pushing, healing, instructing. He made them laugh, and he made them cry. When they left, they said the same thing that so many of his clients said upon leaving: "We have a lot to think about." As always, Ari simply nodded.

Maya appeared a few minutes later. "They left you five thousand dollars, father."

"Good. Go on the Net and buy their albums. I'm curious to hear what they sound like."

"You won't like them!" she laughed.

"Their music? Probably not. But I like them. And I think their next album will be very surprising."

MORAL: If you do something for many years, expect moments of disenchantment.

Your Anxiety Mastery Menu

HIGHLIGHTING: RECOVERY WORK

If anxiety permeates your life, affecting your ability to create, your ability to relate, your ability to dream large, and your ability to live, then you must take your anxiety-management efforts very seriously, as seriously as you would take your efforts to recover from severe depression or an addiction. People who are serious about ending an addiction work their recovery program to keep themselves clean and sober, and you can use the methods and ideas of recovery work to help with anxiety management.

What is a recovery program? It is simply the systematic way in which you deal with a large-size problem. You recover by taking full responsibility for your thoughts and actions, you engage in daily activities that support your goals, and you seek extra support if you can't quite pull off managing the problem on your own. You take your problem seriously and you address it every day as the only item on its own to-do list, making it a top priority in your life.

What might an anxiety recovery program look like? First, you surrender to the fact that anxiety is a part of life and, rather than denying its existence or trying to avoid it at all costs, you look it squarely in the eye and deal with it. Just as an alcoholic in recovery admits that he's an alcoholic, you admit that you get very anxious.

Second, you schedule time every day to practice your anxiety-management tools. You choose one, two, or more strategies and really engage with them. You envision your day, identify situations that tend to make you anxious, and decide how you intend to think and behave in those situations. Are you hoping to get to your studio later in the afternoon but know that you're anxious about going? Decide beforehand how you will deal with that anxiety and then, when the afternoon arrives, deal with that anxiety by using the tools you've practiced and the strategies you've selected.

Third, you maintain awareness of your anxiety issues by paying attention to your thoughts and to your circumstances, watching out for those that trigger anxiety. Fourth, you establish rewards for recovery behaviors. For example, you might reward yourself with some expensive watercolor paper if you managed to deal with your anxiety sufficiently to contact gallery owners. You might reward yourself with a new notebook computer if you managed your anxiety sufficiently to complete your nonfiction book on time. Fifth, you condition yourself to respond to cues in new ways. You train yourself to make a cup of tea rather than reach for the Scotch bottle when anxiety wells up in you.

Your recovery program requires your everyday attention. In the 12-step programs people are encouraged to do "ninety in ninety," that is, to attend ninety self-help meetings in ninety consecutive days. This is the epitome of paying attention. Whatever reason you put forward to miss a day of practicing your anxiety-management tools is unlikely to be a really good reason. If anxiety is such a problem in your life that you've decided to create a recovery program for dealing with it, your mantra should be "I work my recovery program every day."

☑ TO DO

Create your own recovery program for anxiety. You may want to consult the recovery literature to get additional tips and ideas to help you construct your personalized program.

CHAPTER 24

THE ANXIETY OF SUCCESS

More people than you think are ambivalent about success. Maybe you're one of these. Maybe you're happier on the sidelines, in the shadows, or in the background. Maybe you're worried that with success will come an unpleasant array of new challenges and responsibilities. If this worries you, this is anticipatory anxiety: anxiety about something in the future. Your thoughts are weakening your resolve, and your best bet is to deal with this future-oriented anxiety cognitively by replacing your self-sabotaging thoughts with thoughts that serve you. On the whole, it is better to be for success than afraid of success — even if the specter of success makes you anxious.

Perhaps you've gained a significant measure of success, and the anxiety you feel concerns your current reality. This is a very different situation from the first one. This present-oriented anxiety must be dealt with behaviorally: you must actually do something about the new offers coming in, the fan mail, the interview requests, the presents of drugs and sex, the distractions. Reducing this anxiety requires action. Even small successes produce the kinds of situations that typically provoke anxiety: your local newspaper wanting an interview, a small party organized on your behalf with you as the center of attention. Success puts you in the public eye and makes new demands on you, and with that spotlight and those demands comes anxiety.

Both the prospect of success and actual success provoke anxiety. At first glance this might seem surprising. Isn't success exactly what you want? Isn't success a blessing rather than a threat? It turns out that many people aren't positive that they want success and, when they do achieve success, experience it as a very mixed blessing. Often the first year or two of significant success are the most disorienting and difficult years in a creative person's life. With success, all the following can come into play.

You may be afraid that you'll be exposed as a fraud. You may feel trapped by your signature work, the work that everyone now wants and demands from you. You may feel like everyone wants a piece of you and that all day long people are tugging at you. You may regret the compromises you made on the way to stardom, compromises that you hope no one will notice. You may experience a new unreality as people react to you as a celebrity and not as a person. You may have important choices to make, ones that, if you choose incorrectly, will cost you millions and maybe your whole career. And more.

You will want to have mastered some anxiety-management

tools before all this happens! By learning how to reduce your anxiety now, you deal with the anticipatory anxiety that the specter of success produces and you ready yourself for the anxious feelings that actual success, if it arrives, brings. Rather than fearing success and finding small and large ways to avoid it, work on mastering your anxiety so that you can fully embrace the possibility — and the reality — of success.

HEADLINE

The prospect of success and the reality of success both breed anxious feelings. Deal with the former and get ready for the latter by regularly using your anxiety-mastery tools.

☑ TO DO

Have a serious chat with yourself about whether or not you want to become successful as a creative person, remembering that neither choice exempts you from anxiety. You might frame the question in the following loaded way: "Wouldn't I rather deal with the anxiety of success than the anxiety that will come anyway if I contrive never to be successful?"

VOW

I will not avoid success just because I am a little afraid of it.

ARI TEACHING TALE

THE ARRIVAL BY CAMEL OF THE BEST-SELLING AUTHOR

There was a great commotion in the oasis. People were rushing to the western edge, past the great well, past the row of fig trees, to the strip of beaten earth dividing the desert from human habitation. Since his next client wasn't due for a while, Ari wandered in that direction. Almost all the inhabitants of the oasis were there, pointing out toward the desert and straining to see what was happening. From where Ari stood, all he could see were billowing clouds of sand.

As he moved forward the spectacle came into view. A galloping caravan of camels was arriving. It looked like a carnival in motion, the camels sporting colorful canopies, beautiful women waving from some of the canopies, warriors running alongside waving rifles in the air and shouting. Atop the first camel sat a handsome man, indifferent to all the hoopla. Ari recognized him as his next client.

"What is it?" people were crying. "What is it?"

Ari smiled. He turned on his heels and headed home. An hour later his client, one of the world's best-selling suspense writers, arrived. Ari offered the tanned, virile middle-aged man a seat.

"I'm a complete mess," Alexander stated without preamble. "My net worth is $200,000,000, and I'm a complete mess."

"Have a date," Ari said. "And some mint tea. You must have quite a dry throat, coming in like that."

"That entrance! I can't just arrive places — I'm obliged to make entrances. Entrances! Wasn't that the tackiest thing you ever saw? Fit only for a desert Disneyland?"

"You did give people a moment of excitement."

"I aim to please." He poured himself a cup of tea.

"What do these entrances cost?" Ari wondered.

"Some ridiculous amount. I bleed money. My website is practically a nation-state and costs God knows how much. My publicist is on retainer at $15,000 a month. I own seven houses — don't ask me why — and I'm paying money to three ex-wives and some girl-friends." He stopped, made a face. "Why the girlfriends, you ask? Because I fathered some children."

Ari smiled. "You sound very successful. In everything you do, sex included. And I'm guessing you make more money than you spend. So isn't all your woe a bit unseemly and, oh, maybe just posturing?"

Alexander — Alexander the Great, as the tabloids had it — stared at Ari speculatively.

"Some people are cowed by me," he said. "Others retain their sense of personal power by insulting me. I suppose you are one of those?"

Ari shrugged. "I don't doubt that you have your woes, being human. But so far your complaints are silly."

Alexander took a long time in replying. Finally he burst out laughing.

"They are!" he exclaimed. "Of course I take pride in all those women and all those expenses. But I am a mess. Truly I am. May I try to explain myself?"

"Yes," Ari said. "Have some more tea."

Alexander nodded. "I would say that I am a mess in three major areas. First, I am completely manic. Second, I can't get sated. My appetites are completely off the chart. Third, I am so bored by what I write. I get so bored that I hire people to write my novels. I tell them what I want, I oversee it, it's like a Chinese factory. I turn out the cheap running shoes of literature." He looked at Ari. "Maybe you think I'm dying to write 'literature.' I can't say that's the case. Who needs *War and Peace*? I'm completely — unmotivated. If that's the right word. Un-something."

"Did you know that mania is an anxiety state?" Ari said.

"Is it?" Alexander cocked his head and thought about that. "It doesn't feel like anxiety."

"It is. It's a special case of existential anxiety. You are running like mad so as not to notice that life has no meaning. That's why you get so irritated if anything slows you down or gets in your way. You get irritated because you know in a corner of your consciousness that if you were to stop you would come right up against the void. You do get irritated, don't you?"

"I am notorious for my fits of irritability. I am a monster in that regard."

"If you came to a standstill, you would notice all that nothingness. Your whole body is vibrating at some frequency meant to prevent you from coming to that bad resting place."

"I've never thought of myself as an anxious person," he said after some long pondering. "And I'm not — in a traditional sense. But what you're describing... it's dead-on."

Ari nodded. "Oddly enough, the success makes the

underlying dread worse. If you hadn't made it, you might be able to delude yourself by saying, 'When I make it, life will have meaning.' But you have made it, so that rationale won't work. You mentioned Tolstoy a moment ago — he arrived at this exact same place."

"He didn't come up with an answer, did he? He ran away from home to die in a railroad station. He was running — just like me."

"Exactly."

"And I suppose you'll tell me that there's no answer."

"Not at all!" Ari laughed. "Tolstoy didn't have me."

Alexander didn't crack a smile. "So what is the answer?"

"This thinking that you are now doing, it is the road to the answer," Ari said.

"I'm not thinking anything!" Alexander replied. "Nothing coherent. I'm just…taking in your words… and spinning inside."

"You're spinning, yes, but in the direction of an answer."

They sat quietly for fifteen minutes. In such circumstances, fifteen minutes is twice an eternity. It seemed liked hours and hours. Ari sat patiently, watching Alexander think.

"It's beginning to sink in," Alexander said. "It's such a relief to know that I'm anxious. It's quite an amazing revelation, really. I can almost see the outline of answers. I already see that I don't need to make entrances on camels. I can already see what that was all about."

He sat silently for another minute and then snapped his fingers. He appeared to have made a decision. He pulled out a cell phone, dialed, listened, then said into the phone, "Hello, Mark? This is Alexander. I need you to gather a damage-control team. What? Yes, a scandal. What? When?" He shot Ari a glance, then thought for a moment. "Next week, on Monday. I'm not coming right back. I'm...taking my time. What? Where? Maybe I'll be staying here for a bit...in the desert...there's this wise old guy...what? Yes, like Don Juan, only he uses ice water instead of magic mushrooms."

Ari smiled. He waited for Alexander to put his cell phone away and said, "So you're going to confess that you didn't write those recent novels?"

"I am."

"That will prove interesting."

"It will."

They sat quietly.

"More tea?" Ari said.

"Is it possibly time for a Scotch?" Alexander said.

Ari laughed. "It could be. And do you require dancing girls? And sword swallowers? And caviar by the pound?"

Alexander shook his head. "I'd like some quiet time with you. I want to be with this delicious...nonanxiety. I want to get to know it so that I can reproduce it. It's one thing to be quiet sitting here with you in the desert. The second I leave here it won't be so easy. I'm already losing my conviction...."

"Hush," Ari murmured. "Don't worry. That's only another face of your anxiety! It's going to take you a while to recognize all its faces."

Alexander nodded. He shut his eyes and sat quietly. Ari guessed that, whether or not he knew it, Alexander had already begun working on his next novel, one very different from his previous novels and one that he would write all by himself.

MORAL: Anxiety spares no one, not even world-famous authors who arrive by camel.

Your Anxiety Mastery Menu

In Conclusion

The creative process, the creative life, and the human mind provoke anxiety. If you can get a grip on your mind, you will go a long way toward extinguishing much of the anxiety in your life. But life itself presents the kinds of threats and difficulties that make it virtually impossible to eliminate all anxiety. Try to extinguish the portion of your anxiety that it is possible to extinguish, and for the remaining portion, make use of the anxiety-management techniques that I've been describing in these lessons.

None of these techniques will be available to you when you need them simply because you read about them in these lessons, nodded, and had the sure sense that this one or that might work well for you. Rather, you must practice and use them. It is not enough to agree that your self-talk is unhelpful and unfriendly. You must notice what you're saying to yourself, dispute those utterances that don't serve you, and actively substitute more affirmative, useful language. It isn't enough to like the idea of guided imagery or to agree that stress reduction makes sense. You must practice your chosen visualization and your chosen stress-reduction techniques. If you want the results, do the work.

Anxiety is a signal of danger. It's at once a biological and psychological signal, alerting us to the fact that something may be up. But it isn't a terribly accurate signal, as often nothing much is really happening. However, most of us hate the experience of anxiety so much that instead of feeling the anxiety when it hits and looking to see whether the threat is real or significant, we try to wall the experience away. We attempt to defend ourselves against the experience of anxiety rather than examining and handling the threat. By doing so, we lose our ability to see what's provoking the anxiety and our ability to simply dispense with the threat.

Rather than strenuously defending yourself against anxiety, an effort that will prevent you from taking the kinds of risks that the creative process and the creative life demand, accept that anxiety is part of your early-warning system and your genetic inheritance and learn to deal with anxiety rather than avoiding or denying it. If you strive to acquire a more detached, philosophical attitude, work to get a grip on your mind so that you create less anxiety, and master a few anxiety-management tools, you will dramatically reduce your experience of anxiety and effectively handle the portion that remains.

NOTES

Chapter 9. The Anxiety of Compromising

1. Roshi Philip Kapleau, *The Three Pillars of Zen: Teaching, Practice, and Enlightenment* (Norwell, MA: Anchor Press, 1989), 11.
2. Christopher McCullough and Robert Woods Mann, *Managing Your Anxiety: Regaining Control When You Feel Stressed, Helpless, and Alone* (New York: Berkely Publishing, 1994), 210.
3. Stephanie Judy, *Making Music for the Joy of It* (Los Angeles: Tarcher, 1990), 261–62.

Chapter 12. The Anxiety of Thinking

1. Renée Harmon, *How to Audition for Movies and TV* (New York: Walker and Company, 1992).
2. Charles Stroebel, *QR: Quieting Reflex Training for Adults* (New York: Putnam, 1982).
3. Edmund Bourne, *The Anxiety and Phobia Workbook,* 4th ed. (Oakland, CA: New Harbinger, 2005), 79–80.

Chapter 13. The Anxiety of Ruining

1. Stephanie Judy, *Making Music for the Joy of It* (Los Angeles: Tarcher, 1990), 267.
2. Reid Wilson, *Don't Panic: Taking Control of Anxiety Attacks,* 3rd ed. (New York: HarperCollins, 2009), 302–3.

CHAPTER 15. THE ANXIETY OF COMPLETING

1. Roberto Assagioli, *Psychosynthesis: A Collection of Basic Writings* (Amherst, MA: Synthesis Center, 2000).

CHAPTER 17. THE ANXIETY OF EGO BRUISING

1. Douglas Hunt, *No More Fears* (New York: Warner, 1989).
2. Marian Seldes, *The Bright Lights: A Theatre Life* (Milwaukee, WI: Limelight Editions, 1984).

CHAPTER 18. THE ANXIETY OF PERFORMING

1. Stephanie Judy, *Making Music for the Joy of It* (Los Angeles: Tarcher, 1990), 260.
2. Manuel J. Smith, *Kicking the Fear Habit* (New York: Bantam, 1978), 62.

CHAPTER 19. THE ANXIETY OF SELLING

1. Ann Seagrave, *Free from Fears: New Help for Anxiety, Panic & Agorophobia* (New York: Pocket, 1989).

CHAPTER 20. THE ANXIETY OF PROMOTING

1. Eloise Ristad, *A Soprano on Her Head: Right-Side-Up Reflections on Life and Other Performances*, 4th ed. (Boulder, CO: Real People Press, 1981), 162–63.
2. Viktor Frankl, *Psychotherapy and Existentialism* (New York: Simon and Schuster, 1967), 4.
3. Frankl, *Psychotherapy and Existentialism*, 5.

CHAPTER 21. THE ANXIETY OF PROCRASTINATING

1. Sheldon Kopp, *Raise Your Right Hand Against Fear: Extend the Other in Compassion* (New York: Ballantine, 1990).

CHAPTER 22. THE ANXIETY OF WAITING

1. Julian Lieb and D. Jablow Hershman, *Manic Depression and Creativity* (Amherst, New York: Prometheus Books, 1998), 54.

INDEX

ABOUT THE AUTHOR

Eric Maisel, PhD, is the author of thirty books and widely regarded as America's foremost creativity coach. He trains creativity coaches nationally and internationally and provides core trainings for the Creativity Coaching Association. Eric is a columnist for *Art Calendar* magazine and is currently building the fields of meaning coaching and existential cognitive-behavioral therapy (ECBT). His books include *Coaching the Artist Within, Creative Recovery, Fearless Creating, The Van Gogh Blues,* and a score of others. He lives in the San Francisco Bay Area with his family.

His website is www.ericmaisel.com.

NEW WORLD LIBRARY is dedicated to publishing books and other media that inspire and challenge us to improve the quality of our lives and the world.

We are a socially and environmentally aware company, and we strive to embody the ideals presented in our publications. We recognize that we have an ethical responsibility to our customers, our staff members, and our planet.

We serve our customers by creating the finest publications possible on personal growth, creativity, spirituality, wellness, and other areas of emerging importance. We serve New World Library employees with generous benefits, significant profit sharing, and constant encouragement to pursue their most expansive dreams.

As a member of the Green Press Initiative, we print an increasing number of books with soy-based ink on 100 percent postconsumer-waste recycled paper. Also, we power our offices with solar energy and contribute to nonprofit organizations working to make the world a better place for us all

Our products are available
in bookstores everywhere.
For our catalog, please contact:

New World Library
14 Pamaron Way
Novato, California 94949

Phone: 415-884-2100 or 800-972-6657
Catalog requests: Ext. 50
Orders: Ext. 52
Fax: 415-884-2199
Email: escort@newworldlibrary.com

To subscribe to our electronic newsletter, visit
www.newworldlibrary.com

HELPING TO PRESERVE OUR ENVIRONMENT

New World Library uses 100% postconsumer-waste recycled paper for our books whenever possible, even if it costs more. During 2009 this choice saved the following precious resources:

7,205
trees were saved

www.newworldlibrary.com

ENERGY	WASTEWATER	GREENHOUSE GASES	SOLID WASTE
22 MILLION BTU	3 MILLION GAL.	685,000 LB.	200,000 LB.

Environmental impact estimates were made using the Environmental Defense Fund Paper Calculator @ www.papercalculator.org.